The Power of Difference:
From Conflict to Collaboration
in Five Steps

The Power of Difference:
From Conflict to Collaboration
in Five Steps

Dana Morris-Jones

Published by The Delphi Group

Printed in the United States of America

First Printing, 2016

ISBN 978-0-9975328-0-7

The Power of Difference: From Conflict to Collaboration in Five Steps
Written by Dana Z. Morris-Jones
Edited, designed and formatted by Shelagh Aitken
Illustrations by Angela C. Dowd
Cover designed by Angela C. Dowd
Cover based on an idea by Brian Setness

First published in the United States in 2016 by:
The Delphi Group
4 Carter Brook Dr
Scarborough, ME 04074
United States

http://www.thedelphigroup.com

Thanks to my partner John for sharing so much of his insight and experience and for encouraging me to be my best.

Table of Contents

Foreword To the Reader   ix

The Theory Behind the Practical Approach   **1**

Chapter 1 The Nature of Conflict in Organizations   3

Chapter 2 Regarding Human Nature   15

Chapter 3 The Role of Emotions   23

Chapter 4 The Power of Purpose: Creating a Culture of Alignment 33

A Practical Process for Resolving Differences Constructively   **49**

Chapter 5 Prepare—Part One: Understand the Situation   53

Chapter 6 Prepare—Part Two: Analyze the Information for Clues 69

Chapter 7 Prepare—Part Three: Know Yourself, Know Others   81

Chapter 8 Step 2: Engage   97

Chapter 9 Step 3: Diverge   113

Chapter 10 Step 4: Co-Create   135

Chapter 11 Step 5: Agree and Implement   149

Chapter 12 Yes, But...   159

Summary Table: Five Steps for Resolving Differences Constructively 163

Acknowledgments   169

References   171

Additional Recommended Reading   173

Foreword: To The Reader

This book has been "percolating" in my head for at least a decade, but the catalyst that moved me to action was the impact of the many situations my partner, John, and I have encountered in our work. Whether working one-on-one as coaches to an executive, teaching leadership skills to corporate managers, or helping teams become more effective, we have frequently been told about situations in which managers and leaders felt confounded by an inability to resolve differences constructively. Most realized that these ongoing disagreements were having a negative impact, not only on everyone directly involved but on the organization as a whole. They very much wanted to find solutions but were at a loss as to how to do that.

The kinds of disagreements we were hearing about were not the kind that would resolve on their own if one person would just back down. This was not "the guy in the next cubicle chews his gum too loud." Rather, we were hearing about issues that were affecting morale, productivity, and the ability of teams or whole divisions to be as effective as they could be to be able to contribute to the organization's success. These were complex issues that involved many people and many legitimate concerns and viewpoints. Not resolving them often led to complicated "work-around" accommodations, delayed schedules, poor decisions, and missed opportunities. Furthermore, the best solutions were not likely to come about as a result of one person saying "my way or the highway"; they required people to work together to reach solutions that would benefit everyone, i.e. "collaboration."

While the notion of "collaboration" has become ubiquitous, most people have not been exposed to the skills needed to achieve it. The ability to engage in collaborative problem solving, particularly when the outcome may have a significant impact on those involved, requires a combination of attitudes, beliefs, and learned skills. We wanted to be able to give our clients all of these things along with a solid set of reference materials. There are many books and articles about conflict resolution but few, we found, that tackle the kinds of issues we were hearing about and even fewer that teach practical hands-on techniques for gaining the requisite skill sets. We have tried to provide those with this book.

It is also worth noting here that these methods are not for every disagreement encountered in an organization. The processes we advocate are time and energy consuming, and are most justified for situations in which there is much at stake. On the other hand, once these methods are practiced and mastered, they can be beneficial for even less impactful situations. We believe that organizations gain a significant competitive edge when these practices become ingrained as part of the culture.

We also recognize that there are instances in which time simply does not permit a lengthy process. Nonetheless, we believe it is almost always advantageous to adopt some of the attitudes and mental skill sets offered here. There is no guarantee that the very best outcomes will always be achieved; however, we can guarantee that favorable outcomes are far more likely as a result of using this approach than not.

Why Dealing With Differences in Organizations is Important

Modern society is, to a large extent, built on the existence of complex organizations which, arguably, manage and produce everything that makes civilization possible. We simply cannot live without them. Yet, by their very nature, differences are an inherent quality of organizations. This is true because in order to do what they do, they must include some diversity of function—even the simplest include some form of design, production, sales, and administration—and some hierarchical levels of management and oversight. Differences frequently evolve into competitions for power of various sorts, e.g. influence over decision making, resources and individual ranking. These differences can be the source of excellence, adaptation, and innovation, or they can be the cause of inefficiency, stagnation, and failure, depending on how they are addressed and managed. Yet managing differences constructively is not a skill that comes naturally to most humans. It is not surprising that a recent Stanford University study (*2013 Executive Coaching Survey*, Stanford University with The Miles Group) found that "Conflict Management Skills" was the highest ranked response in answer to the question "What areas are CEO's Getting Coached In?" The importance of this set of skills as a necessary element of organizational success cannot be overstated.

A Word about Language

One of the challenges of doing this work and writing about it is finding the most useful and appropriate words to use. "Conflict" and "conflict resolution" are the most common terms used by the people who are practitioners in the field of mediation and facilitation. The *Dictionary of Conflict Resolution* (1999) defines conflict as "Disagreement or incompatibility, derived from the Latin, *conflictus*, meaning 'to strike together'."

We think it is noteworthy that the first part of the definition seems to imply that conflict is no more serious or potentially destructive than an everyday disagreement or incompatibility; in another word, a slight difference. Yet the Latin root implies a rather violent process. And in fact, when we ask people what they think of when they hear the word conflict, most offer words that connote violence and fear, like "war" and "danger."

We want people to approach these situations with the belief that they can be resolved constructively, without being fearful that they may do harm to themselves or others in the process, and that there is no need to avoid dealing with issues directly. Since many people have a "fight or flight" response, we felt it would be most useful to use a word with a more neutral connotation.

Another word we could have used is "dispute". The same dictionary discusses the word "dispute" at length to distinguish it from "conflict", saying "A dispute exists only after a claim is made and rejected". This implies that there is a procedural element and we have found that most people believe "dispute" has to do with the law and with issues that are to be litigated. Again, this is far from what we want our audience to be thinking about, as legal approaches to organizational differences are typically a last resort, as they should be.

Another word we considered was "disagreement", defined as "having a difference of opinion or inconsistent views." While close to what we mean, "disagreement" seems to imply a very simple difference rather than a complex one.

The word "difference" is used by most of us in a casual, everyday way, to describe ways in which things are dissimilar from one another. Roget's *Thesaurus* lists "disagreement," "difficulty," and "misunderstanding" as synonyms, and further references "difference of opinion," "agreement to disagree," "variance," "division," "dividedness," "polarity of opinion," "cross-purposes," "disparity," "divergence," and "gap." All of these words are consistent with the meaning we intend: people having views or preferences or interests that are inconsistent with one another's but not irresolvable. The term "difference" is the one we have chosen to use most frequently throughout the book.

We want to make a clear distinction between differences that cannot be changed, like gender, age, race, or ethnicity, and those that can, like perceptions, beliefs, and interpretations. The former, which are generally implied by the term "diversity" undoubtedly influence the latter in many ways. Whether differences are immutable or amenable to change, we contend that they are never bad in and of themselves and are always a potential source of rich and creative processes when managed constructively. It is that process on which we hope to shed light.

Who the Book is For and How to Use It

This book has been written from the perspective of someone who is directly involved in a difference that needs to be resolved, but we also imagine it being used by anyone who is indirectly involved and in a position to intervene in some way. We believe that anyone who works in an organization of any size larger than one can benefit from the approaches we are teaching. The audience for whom this content is most useful is anyone with responsibility for managing others or leading or participating in work that involves working across organizational boundaries and is complex. The examples we cite include differences among groups or individuals, peers within or across organizational boundaries, bosses and direct reports. We think it will also be particularly useful for those who act as third parties to assist others, including Human Resource professionals, Organization Development consultants, corporate trainers, mediators and employee assistance staff.

The book consists of two sections. The first provides a context and makes the case for the relationship between organizational success and the constructive resolution of differences. The four chapters in Part One discuss the nature of conflict in organizations with many specific examples, explore how human nature neither condemns us to be completely selfish or selfless creatures, but allows us to choose the most effective behaviors for the situation, explores the role of emotions, and outlines a specific kind of organizational culture in which collaborative approaches to resolving differences are most likely to thrive. These chapters can stand alone as a philosophic treatise that sets the stage for the more concrete and skills-based second part.

The chapters in Part Two correspond to our model of constructive resolution of differences: Prepare, Engage, Diverge, Co-create, Agree and Implement. Each of these chapters describes the specific attitudes, skills, and behaviors needed to execute the step with many helpful examples and stories. We have devoted three chapters to the first step (Prepare) because without carefully laying the groundwork for following steps, the entire process is far less likely to succeed.

The final chapter is an attempt to respond to many of the "Yes, but…?" questions that may have popped into readers' minds as they read the first eleven.

The Theory Behind the Practical Approach

"There is nothing so practical as a good theory."—Kurt Lewin

This quote is often attributed to Kurt Lewin, a pioneer in Social Psychology and arguably the father of modern theory related to constructive conflict resolution. In keeping with Dr. Lewin's sentiment, without theory, the approach we offer to resolving differences would be nothing more than the product of our hopes and beliefs. Though not rendering it without merit, building a methodology on our experience alone would be difficult to defend.

We offer, therefore, conceptual and theoretical tenets in four areas: the nature of conflict in organizations, human nature, the role of emotions and behavior as it relates to conflict, and the power of purpose and alignment in organizations. These ideas, taken together, have shaped our thinking to a very large degree.

You may decide to skip this first part of the book and go straight to the practical methods described in the second part, "A Practical Approach for Resolving Differences Constructively." If you find yourself wondering what the basis is for the recommendations in the second part of the book, you may want to double back to this first part.

Chapter 1

The Nature of Conflict in Organizations

Anyone who has ever worked in an organization can readily describe situations in which conflicts have had considerable negative impact: on the organization itself as well as the groups or individuals directly or even indirectly involved. Many fewer people can describe organizational conflicts that actually lead to enhanced outcomes, both for the organization as a whole as well as the individuals. We believe enhanced outcomes are possible. In fact, our experience in working with dozens of organizations has taught us that the practices that underlie constructive management of differences in organizations also lead to greater effectiveness overall.

Some of these situations may sound familiar:

> *Barbara, a talented woman responsible for a large staff and a considerable budget, was clearly at the end of her rope. For months she had been trying to find a way to get the message across to her boss, the CEO, that she simply could not continue to deliver the expected results with the available resources. She had analyzed the numbers, juggled assignments and reporting structures, proposed multiple alternatives and sent memo after memo, with no results. She felt disrespected, ignored, taken advantage of and just plain angry. She was short-tempered with her staff, which was taking a toll on everyone.*

***

> *A rapidly growing catering business hired a new executive chef to oversee everything in the kitchen, which included developing new menus, choosing vendors and ordering food. One person reporting to the new chef, who had been responsible for these functions, had imagined that she would be next in line to be the top chef. While the conflict between them was not overt, every change introduced by the new chef created discord.*

The heads of two departments, both ultimately responsible for delivering and installing new software, were locked in escalating battles revolving around scheduling, deadlines and shared resources. As both grew more frustrated with the situation and with one another, they communicated less, the problems increased, their respective staffs fell in line behind them and against one another and, hardly a surprise, both quality and productivity declined in both departments.

***

The advertising sales representatives for a magazine, whose job it was to sell as many pages of advertising as possible, were always complaining that there were never enough good new marketing ideas and value-added packages being created by the marketing/creative services team. The creative services team believed the sales reps were promising unreasonable and too labor-intensive services, leaving little time to come up with new ideas. This had been going on for so long that neither team really expected anything to change; they were all perpetually frustrated and annoyed.

***

The new CEO of a long-established health-care agency had an ambitious agenda for redefining services based on the changing demographics and marketplace in the service area. A few of the longest standing board members had different ideas about the services they should provide and the relationship the agency should have with the community. They formed a coalition to block the CEO's actions.

Each of these is an example of differences that have become conflicts. They may have gone underground, manifested in frayed tempers, frustrated ambitions, excessive turnover, absenteeism and a culture of resignation. In some cases, they have developed into overt aggression. These organizations may survive, but they will fail to thrive. They will gradually become places that people would rather not be and that do not achieve the results to which they aspire.

This scenario is not uncommon but it *is* avoidable. We have the knowledge and tools to prevent these negative outcomes. We can do more than just prevent them. We have the ability to harness the energy that fuels the negativity and channel it toward desirable results. These outcomes can include organizational transformation and success for the enterprise and all who choose to participate in it.

The keys to such success lie in the combined concepts of organizational culture; alignment of values, norms, and practices; and the development of skills that support collaboration and constructive resolution of differences. Individually, none of the ideas is new. Each is powerful, in and of itself, for mapping out processes that help people interact with one another in ways that lead to positive outcomes. Together, they have the ability to transform organizations into exceptionally productive, innovative enterprises with the very real competitive advantage of a wholly committed workforce.

What Makes Organizational Conflict So Challenging in the Current Environment?

While the presence of conflict in organizations is not anything new, it has become more pervasive in recent years. It is closer to the surface, potentially more difficult to manage, and more destructive. There are several factors that contribute to this trend and are simply "givens" in the world in which we live.

Flat Organization Structures

Because technology has increased the availability of information, up down and across, today's updated organizations have eliminated layers of management. This provides the benefit of lower costs and greater empowerment of employees, who are closer to the work and to the customer. An unintended negative consequence is that employees at all levels now take greater responsibility for decision making and for coordinating tasks across boundaries. This can generate conflict which employees are ill-prepared to address constructively.

Complexity and Interdependence

Organizations now engage in webs of multiple inter-related products, services and processes. They serve many markets, relying on a plethora of vendors and other external stakeholders. Organizational structures often reflect this complexity, with great interdependence across functional, vertical, and horizontal boundaries. Role confusion occurs frequently. Organization charts do not capture the true nature of who reports to whom, who relies on whom, how input must be sought, information exchanged, and how decisions are made. All of these transactions depend on relationships, constant problem solving, and resolving of day-to-day differences in which virtually everyone is involved. The potential for conflict is enormous and perpetual.

In addition, organizations have taken on a more "organic" nature, routinely shifting and evolving to adapt to the continuous changes taking place around them. As this occurs, systemic problems and their underlying root causes are exposed, making them potentially more amenable to change but also making solutions dependent on the interaction of multiple people, perspectives, and variables.

Greater Diversity in the Workforce

It is not unusual for teams to include individuals of many different nationalities and ethnic backgrounds, not to mention the diversity of gender, age, race, and religion among those born and raised in the U.S. This heterogeneity extends to fundamental assumptions and values regarding how we should interact; what words, tone of voice, and gestures mean; and how we should approach differences. While diversity in the workplace is a positive reflection of greater tolerance and acceptance, it also makes resolving differences more complex and difficult.

Greater Emphasis on "Me/I" than "We/Us"

Human beings have two fundamental yet potentially opposing drives. The first is the need to feel unique, separate, powerful, and in control (me/I). The other is the need to be in relationship with and accepted by others (we/us). When these drives are relatively balanced, individuals are able to advocate for themselves as well as give way to others either to preserve relationships, or for the greater good. Recent generations have earned the title "me generation" because they seem to lean more heavily to the "me/I" side of the equation. Whether the difference is generational or not, large portions of the workforce seem to be less open to other viewpoints and more apt to stubbornly cling to a desire to "win" or "be true to myself". In addition, some seem less likely to willingly sacrifice a short-term gain for a longer term, more enduring or comprehensive solution. When the majority of people operate this way, differences constantly get escalated. Resolving them can seem almost impossible.

The Pace of Life

Though some would say that organizational life has always been fast paced, we sense a new level of frenzy, not only in people's professional lives but in their personal lives as well. There is little time for reflection and very little patience. This works against thoughtful conflict resolution in obvious ways.

Conflict in Organizations is Inevitable— And That's Not Bad

All of these underlying factors are impossible to eliminate, thus making the potential for destructive conflict an inevitable part of organizational life. Though that is true, we do not believe that differences are inherently bad. We believe that differences are a necessary ingredient in an organization's effectiveness and adaptability. Just as pain in the body is a signal that something needs attention, even unpleasant conflict in an organization can act as an indicator that something needs to change. If addressed skillfully, conflict represents an opportunity. Of course, also like pain, if ignored, the situation may get worse.

Conflict in organizations generally involves multiple causes and issues. It can exist among individuals; within or between groups; between an individual and a group; between groups; or among multiple groups. Conflict can occur between a boss and subordinate, between co-workers within a team or counterparts in different groups or departments. It can cross hierarchies and functions, and involve issues related to resources, roles, expectations, processes, objectives, priorities, outcomes, politics, power, egos, and even values. Frequently, conflict includes many of these.

Organizational conflict rarely occurs in a vacuum. It is related to and impacted by the system and the culture in which it takes place. Organizations that acknowledge their complexity and interdependence, and emphasize the importance of collaboration, are more likely to support thoughtful and constructive conflict resolution practices. This intent, while a tremendous advantage, is not a safeguard against the potential for destructive conflict. It is merely a foundation on which to build specific policies, practices, and skills. Imagine then, how disruptive and costly conflict can become in organizations that do not overtly endorse collaboration or covertly subvert it by sustaining cultures that reward competitive, finger-pointing, non-collaborative behavior.

It is naïve to think there are organizations that are so perfectly aligned that conflict does not exist. On the contrary, just as in any healthy relationship, acknowledgment of differences and effective conflict resolution practices enable all parties to know that they can be fully themselves and still co-exist. An absence of overt conflict suggests that either differences are "going underground" and being played out covertly, or the environment is so oppressive that individuals do not feel comfortable expressing their true beliefs and opinions. In either case, what is lost is the give and take of opinions that leads to high-quality decision making and the full utilization of the talent represented by the people the organization valued enough to hire.

Building an organization that supports constructive conflict resolution requires a multi-layered approach. The foundation must be a culture that supports collaboration through a clear articulation of values, purpose, vision, and strategy. The next layer includes the network of practices and policies that aligns with the cultural foundation and gives rise to and rewards behaviors that are consistent with it. Finally, all participants must be taught the skills that are necessary to resolve differences in collaborative and constructive ways.

The Cost of Unmanaged Conflict

This is no simple, overnight quick fix! It requires a dedicated, systematic, and sustained effort. So, is it worth the effort? While it may be impossible to accurately measure all of the tangible and intangible ways that poorly managed conflict can rob an organization of value, it is relatively easy to list all the possible ways in which persistent unresolved conflict can have a negative impact on an organization's bottom line.

Time

At the most basic level, unresolved conflict takes time; time for employees to engage directly in arguing, bickering, and going around and around the same issue without resolution. More indirectly, time is lost when those engaged in non-productive conflict worry about it, think about it, or talk about it to others who are not directly involved, instead of keeping their mind on the work in front of them.

"Work Around's"

A frequent consequence of unresolved conflict is people making pretzel-like accommodations to avoid having to deal with the person or the issue involved. They may ask to be re-assigned, hand tasks off to others less appropriate, and make less-than-ideal staffing choices to avoid having to deal directly with the conflict.

Decision Making

Rather than address the conflict as a problem to be solved, getting input from all those who have expertise or insight, conflict often leads people to exclude others inappropriately, leading to less-than-ideal decisions. At worst, persistent unresolved conflict can lead people to make intentional decisions to harm a person they see as an adversary rather than a colleague. Such decisions are rarely in the best interest of the organization.

Morale and Loyalty

Workplaces with an abundance of unresolved conflict are not particularly enjoyable places to work. Eventually, motivation, enthusiasm, morale, and general job satisfaction are affected. Employee loyalty and commitment decline, ultimately resulting in higher-than-desirable turnover, a costly byproduct.

Compliance Rather Than Commitment

Employees who are embattled and embittered are more likely to develop an attitude of compliance, doing the minimum rather than taking initiative or seeing themselves as being invested in the success of the organization. This is a tremendous loss to any organization as employee commitment is often a significant source of competitive edge.

Stress and Distress

Everyone knows the cost of stress in the workplace, including decreased productivity, a myriad of health issues, and the concomitant increased cost of lost work days and health insurance costs. Persistent unresolved conflict is one of the most significant contributors to stress in the workplace.

Outward Image and Customer Relations

Organizations that are fraught with unresolved conflict are more likely to be seen by customers, vendors, and others who interact with them routinely as disorganized, with different parts of the organization being uninformed about what other parts are doing. When customers hear an employee complaining about other people and departments, they have good reason to believe they are not getting the service they expect.

A History of Building Collaborative Cultures in Organizations

"Resolving conflict" and "managing differences" in organizations has been a topic addressed by organization development (OD) professionals for decades. The foundation for OD's approach to conflict can be found in the early works of social scientists Kurt Lewin (1948), Morton Deutsch (1973), Pruitt and Rubin (1975), Blake and Mouton (1984), and Johnson and Johnson (1989). The orientation of these authors, and the multitude of OD consultants who have worked to help strengthen their client organizations, is that conflict, when well managed, is a source of positive energy, creativity, and healthy relationships. Managing differences fairly and effectively, whether they occur across horizontal or vertical lines, between groups or within groups or between individuals, is, in fact, a tremendously important part of what managers must do well.

The implicit assumption underlying this approach to managing differences in the work place is that everyone who is part of an organization is, in one way or another, dependent upon everyone else; everyone benefits when positive relationships are preserved. Furthermore, the strength of any organization is, in part, a function of how well it makes use of its resources, including the diversity of perspectives of all of its members. The best decisions are made when people are able and willing to communicate and collaborate across organizational boundaries, applying the best thinking of diverse orientations, rather than working separately in silos. It is not necessarily easy or expedient to take the time and make the effort to understand others' ideas, but doing so almost always leads to better solutions.

Finally, everyone who works for an organization stands to benefit when the entire organization succeeds. There is an inherent shared interest in the overall success of the enterprise. Given this orientation, it is a very short leap to suggest that managing differences effectively is everyone's responsibility. Doing so is an essential and integral part of what makes organizations successful.

Competition, Collaboration, and Conflict

My children grew up at a time when every child who made it from one end of the pool to the other during the Saturday morning swim-meets got a ribbon—not a blue ribbon, but a ribbon nonetheless. The thinking was that their self-esteem might be damaged if they were not praised for every effort. Perhaps some of this trend persists, but it has certainly been challenged by those who believe that motivation and achievement come not only from confidence built on self-esteem but also from knowledge of one's strengths and pride in the ability to do some things better than other people. In other words, competition can be healthy, not only for our economy but for individuals as well. And whether we like it or not, competition is inextricably woven into our American culture.

Yet, at the same time, we seem to have entered an age in which the notion of collaboration is ubiquitous. U.S. Intelligence Agencies are urged to collaborate in order to "connect the dots" to prevent terrorist activity; state and local agencies are asked to collaborate (and one step further—consolidate) to achieve efficiency and cost savings. Within organizations, functional departments must collaborate to become more innovative, agile, and responsive to customers. The very word "collaboration" has taken on a motherhood-and-apple-pie connotation.

How do these two concepts jibe with one another? Is it possible to become collaborative when individuals, groups, and whole organizations have been programmed and rewarded to compete? If so, how do we do it? And is collaboration really right for every situation? How do we determine where it is useful and where it might not be?

We believe that there are definite benefits to becoming collaborative in some situations, particularly those that are characterized by the following:

- The entity as a whole (i.e. nation, state, agency, organization, community, family) clearly has something to gain as a result of all members working together.

- The members care about the well-being of the whole and are likely to profit in some way by its success.

- There are potentially elegant and creative paths or strategies that benefit the whole as well as most of the members in the long term.

Even when these conditions are present, it may not be an easy thing to turn a traditionally competitive set of relationships into collaborative ones. One sure-fire way to guarantee failure is to continue to reward "winners" without also compensating collaborative activities and outcomes. Although difficult, it is possible for organizations to create a balance between encouraging healthy internal competition and maintaining a culture that rewards loyalty to the organization as a whole.

To do this takes more than well-thought-out policies: It takes a set of skills and behaviors that may not come naturally to most. These include all of the skills associated with resolving differences and managing conflict constructively.

The Benefits of Collaborative Culture

We have outlined the negative impacts of unmanaged conflict. The qualities that characterize many organizations today—increasing complexity, flatter and less clearly bounded structures, greater diversity—point clearly to the need for collaborative behaviors to replace competitive ones. Happily, organizational cultures of collaboration that support constructive conflict resolution practices produce much greater benefits than simply avoiding adverse impacts. When everyone participates in the constructive processes we will outline in the following chapters, the results include:

- Enduring, high-quality solutions to issues and problems;

- Solutions that represent creative, innovative, out-of-the-box thinking;

- Employees who feel respected and know that their opinions matter;

- Strong, collaborative relationships throughout the organization;

- A workplace that reflects the synergy of an aligned and committed workforce dedicated to the success of the enterprise.

Chapter 2

Regarding Human Nature

Can We Really Co-Exist?

People have been thinking for centuries about conflict, human nature, and whether we can co-exist without destroying ourselves. There has always been speculation about the true nature of human beings. Are we "naturally" aggressive, competitive, and selfish, as Thomas Hobbes argued in the 18th century? Are we primarily motivated by our desire to dominate and be in control, even at the cost of peaceful co-existence and community? Or are we, as Rousseau posited, primarily peace-loving and cooperative, motivated by a desire for connectedness and peaceful society?[1]

Game Theory Explains Human Behavior

In the 1950's, economists attempted to explain human nature in a way that could predict behavior. They devised an experiment called Prisoner's Dilemma, a game in which subjects were assigned the role of one of two prisoners who were being held for the same crime.[2] The prisoners had two options: 1) they could choose to "defect" by saying they knew that the other person committed the crime and they themselves were innocent; or 2)

---

1   Thomas Hobbes and Jean-Jacques Rousseau used their presumptions about human nature to support their opposing views regarding appropriate forms of governance. Hobbes believed that civilization would prevail only if governments forced individuals to cooperate for the greater good; Rousseau believed that governments' attempts to exert control over essentially peace-loving, benign human beings would interfere with those civilized tendencies.

2   Merril Flood and Melvin Dresher of the RAND Corporation are credited with formalizing the Prisoner's Dilemma game.

they could "cooperate" by saying that neither knew anything about the crime. If both defected, both would be charged. If one defected and the other behaved cooperatively, the defector would be released and the other prisoner charged. If both co-operated, they both would go free.

The choice in the game is a pragmatic, not a moral one: What is the most rational choice for either individual? The game mirrors any situation in which there is a tempting reward for doing something that is in one's own self-interest and clearly not in the interest of the common good.

Initially, the game was run for one trial with many different players. The results were almost always the same: One or both players defected. People acted on their prediction that the other person would surely defect; the only rational thing to do was to protect themselves by also defecting. This resulted in the worst-case outcome, with both being charged. Despite the neg-ative outcome, defection seemed to the players to be the only rational decision; cooperation appeared to be irrational. Econo-mists concluded that when confronted with the choice between cooperation and perceived self-protection, people would in-variably choose the self-protective strategy even when damag-ing to another person and potentially damaging to themselves.

Why then, some asked, are there so many examples of coop-erative behavior in the real human world? They continued to devise new experiments in a field that came to be known as "game theory," the goal of which broadened beyond simply predicting behavior to trying to discover strategies that would "win" regardless of the other player's action. In the 1970's other scientists, including biologists and political scientists, started to use game theory to test out their own theories of human behavior. With the aid of computers, they were now able to run the game repeatedly with the same players. They began to observe something very different when the game was run over and over again. Instead of simply choosing a move based on their presumption of the other player's next move, players could anticipate the other player's behavior over time. When that was the case, a new strategy, or pattern of choices, emerged which consistently won. They called the strategy Tit-for-Tat.

Tit-for-Tat consisted of the following decision rules: 1) begin with a cooperative move; 2) do whatever the other player did the last time; 3) return to a cooperative move the next time. It was described by Robert Axelrod, a political scientist who ran a tournament of games played by computer, as being "nice, retaliatory, forgiving, and clear" in a strategy that models niceness but discourages the other side from taking advantage of that niceness. Furthermore, the longer a pair of individuals interacted, the greater the chance that Tit-for-Tat emerged.

Tit-for-Tat came to be understood as a mechanism for generating cooperation; it depends on stable, repetitive, and long-term relationships, e.g. relationships that are *interdependent* in some way. Examples of it can be found in the behavior of many different kinds of animals, including human beings. Apes and people share food, communal hunting was the general rule among hunter-gatherer societies, we band together in things called organizations to maximize our productivity. In each case, people give up some degree of immediate short-term self-interest in exchange for the longer term benefits of cooperation. Where long-term relationships exist, people behave toward one another with *reciprocal altruism*—that is, we instinctively follow the rule that "one good turn deserves another" or "I'll scratch your back if you scratch mine." In the end, it is not cooperation for cooperation's sake but rather cooperation for the good of all. In fact, the efficacy of Tit-for-Tat demonstrates that there is no contradiction between cooperative behavior and self-interest...*cooperation is self-interest in the context of long-lasting, interdependent relationships.*

Social scientists and mathematicians entered into the contest to find a strategy that mirrored the real world and would be stable over time and continue to win over all other strategies. Between the 1980's and the late 90's, several groups of mathematicians took up the challenge to find the perfect strategy that would generate a perpetually winning condition in the real world.[3] With the use of computers and statistically driven probabilities, a succession of strategies emerged, involving ever more frequent cooperation. Even with the entrance of social scientists and mathematicians, no perfect simulation has emerged. One point is, however, consistently clear in all of the winning patterns of behavior: Cooperation is necessary for conflict resolution and it is still the most difficult thing for people to do in the midst of conflict.[4]

It would be an omission not to mention that there is a potential dark side to Tit-for-Tat. If one side chooses a retaliatory move and the other side continues to retaliate, never returning to a cooperative move, it does not take long for it to become a downward cycle of defection and retaliation; witness the Hatfields and McCoys, the continuing violence between Israelis and Palestinians, and, in some organizations we know, the inability of Marketing/Sales Departments and Production to work together collaboratively.

In the world of game theory, Tit-for-Tat continued to be challenged as being unable to explain what happens in the real world, where, in fact, cooperators and defectors both exist. Tit-for-Tat only wins when players are engaged for multiple rounds in which both sides ultimately learn that cooperation is the best strategy. If one player decides to change to a different strategy or defects by mistake, the game can quickly deteriorate into a downward cycle of retaliation.

What Does It Mean?

How can we apply these experiments to our behavior in the world? What does it mean for how we, as human beings, can

---

3   Nowak, M. A., May, R. M. and Sigmund, K. 1995. "The arithmetics of mutual help," *Scientific American 272*: 50–55.

4   A much more detailed account of the history and lessons of game theory can be found in *The Origins of Virtue* by Matthew Ridley, Viking Penguin, 1996.

(and in fact, for the most part, do) create a world in which co-operation prevails? The lessons of game theory suggest that the most successful strategy in the real world rests on a number of principles or assumptions:

- A long-term perspective is required; always assume that there is the greatest potential for your own success when there is mutual, long-term success.

- All behavior is reciprocal, i.e. other's behavior is impacted by yours and yours by theirs.

- It is prudent to remember past behavior of others; those who have cooperated in the past are more likely to cooperate in the future.

- Modeling forgiveness can impact other's behavior, making it more likely that they will learn to cooperate.

These principles and strategies are neither naively cooperative nor protectively defensive; they are not even moralistic—they are pragmatic. It is not about being generous or accommodating or compassionate; it is about doing what is in the best interest of yourself as well as the larger entity, whether it be a family, an organization, a state, a nation, or the world. It is simply about what works!

The larger lessons truly reflect good common sense. Look out for yourself *and* be cognizant of the fact that what is good for any group of which you are a member is most likely to also be good for you. Factor in the reality of reciprocity. Remember, most people are hard-wired to remember how they have been treated by others and are likely to respond in kind. Finally, everyone has the power to shape other people's behavior by making choices about how we treat them…a little like the old "golden rule."

A Real World Organizational Example

Within organizations, it is not difficult to identify ways in which all members ultimately depend on one another for their own success as well as the success of the whole. It only requires that one take the long view.

> Sam had been the associate editor of the daily newspaper for over five years. Management decided that the job was too large for one person and hired another manager to oversee the administrative, day-to-day coordination of the paper. Sam, confused and furious, believed that the message was that he had not been doing a good job. He felt he was being demoted and believed the change would be negatively received by the staff.
>
> The arrival of Rob, the new managing editor, did little to improve Sam's mood. Rob and Sam were to work together closely to direct the staff, edit all submissions and close the paper every day. Sam could barely bring himself to look at Rob directly, let alone work with him to sort out their respective roles and begin to build a cooperative relationship. Neither could he hide his feelings from his staff who were bewildered and disheartened.
>
> Working with Sam, the editor-in-chief, Sam and Rob's boss, and ultimately, the entire staff of the paper, we were able to help Sam shift his focus from concerns about his own role as if it was independent of the whole, to the larger focus on the long-term good for the paper. With this new perspective, we were able to help Sam and Rob cooperate to identify and agree on three key areas:
>
> • Individual responsibilities;
>
> • Practices they would put in place; and
>
> • Procedures to work together to resolve their differences and blend their styles.
>
> Of course this did not magically occur overnight, nor did it instantly alleviate Sam's negative feelings about the

change and how he felt about how he had been treated. It took many months for the relationship between the two managers to smooth out. However, Sam's concern for the well-being of the staff and the health of the paper itself convinced him to put his feelings aside for the sake of the larger, long-term outcome. Ultimately, the paper thrived and all employees in the newsroom, including Sam and Rob, benefited.

Taking the long view of human history, one can find endless examples of both peaceful cooperation and destructive competition. Is it enough to tilt the balance toward cooperation by simply embracing and applying the lessons derived from game theory? We would submit that this is a necessary but not sufficient condition. The acknowledgment of interdependency and a willingness to take the long view is the first step in building a foundation for constructive resolution of differences. But it is only the first step and it may be the easiest. The next ones take more than a leap of faith; they take an established set of practices and many skills.

Key Learning Points

- Game theory illustrates how cooperative behavior benefits individuals when there is a level of interdependence with the other person(s) involved and the relationship extends over a period of time.

- One particular pattern of behavior involving continuous cooperation while also signaling a willingness to retaliate if necessary (called Tit-for-Tat) results in the best collective outcomes.

- It is possible for people to get stuck in a downward spiral of mutually retaliatory behavior if the pattern is abandoned. This can result in escalating levels of conflict that are difficult to end.

- Application of this behavioral pattern to real differences involves assuming a long-term perspective, modeling cooperation and forgiveness, and being willing and able to retaliate only once when the other person retaliates, then returning to cooperation.

- Adopting this pattern of behavior is pragmatic. It is the best strategy to bring about outcomes that are good for oneself as well as for the greater good.

Chapter 3

The Role of Emotions

We've seen that it is in our own best interests to act cooperatively and rationally to resolve our differences. Why then do we so often engage in irrational and uncooperative behavior? Without a doubt, the answer lies in the reality that we are not only rational beings, but also emotional ones. That is why we must consider the role of emotions in resolving differences.

Emotions, like differences, are neither good nor bad in and of themselves. It is how they are managed that allows them to play a positive and constructive role or causes them to become the cause of a derailed and potentially destructive process.

The capacity to experience emotion is a fundamental human quality; one that, arguably, enhances our lives and relationships. When expressed appropriately, shared feelings have the potential to generate human connection, compassion, forgiveness and other positive reactions. When this happens, they can move the process of resolving differences forward in a very positive way. They also have the potential to generate responses such as defensiveness and fear when they are perceived as potentially dangerous or disruptive. When this happens, the process can easily and quickly deteriorate.

We cannot, and would not want to, lessen our emotional experience or our capacity to relate to another's emotional experience. We can and should learn to express emotions in a way that contributes to positive human interactions.

In this chapter, we will explore what is known about human emotions, what they are and what functions they serve, and suggest how we can manage them so that they contribute to, rather than impair, our ability to make good decisions in situations involving conflict.

Understanding Emotions

Historically, psychologists have defined emotions as a cluster of several phenomena, including subjective experience, physiological reactions, cognitive reactions, expressive (non-verbal) reactions such as a smile or a sneer, and expressed, overt behavior such as screaming or embracing someone. There are several different theories, however, about the relationship and causality among these factors and the functions that they serve in producing what we think of as emotions or feelings. Do we feel fear only as a result of seeing something that is to be feared, because we have information from prior experience that identifies the situation as dangerous, or because our body begins to shake and our hands get sweaty? We might all agree that it is probably all of these things. But what of the situation in which our fear reaction is unwarranted and leads us to take actions that are not in our own best interest, e.g. yelling at a co-worker? How should we make sense of that and, more importantly, how can we get better at accurately assessing situations in order to react more appropriately?

Neuroscience, the study of human brain function, has given us a new lens through which to view the role of emotion in decision making. Because of the way our brains are structured, emotional reactions to external stimuli may not get transmitted to the regions of the brain that employ complex processing of data. Rather, we experience them as physical symptoms, e.g. churning in the stomach, jaw tightening, lump in the throat, and react in a primitive way, fight or flight. The primitive, least sophisticated part of the brain is called the amygdala. It's a small, almond-shaped structure at the base of the cortex that acts as a rapid processor of sensory information and a coordinator of a variety of physical systems. It serves to alert us, in multiple ways, to situations in which we may need to act quickly to protect ourselves. Physiological events occur in response to the stimulus without any higher processing that might involve consideration of past experience, values and beliefs, lessons learned or multiple hypotheses regarding the nature of the situation. Behaviors based purely on these physiological hap-penings are not informed by any sort of appraisal or judgment.

Fortunately, we are blessed with the ability to process stimuli in a much more sophisticated way using the part of our brain called the orbitofrontal cortex, or frontal lobes. Here, in the part of the brain located just behind the forehead, we have the ability to apply abstract concepts such as reason and values to assess situations and make decisions that take these into account, along with what we have learned from our own experience and from cultural norms.

Taken together, these parts of our brain help us to use the in-formation about external stimuli that may include important alerts about potential challenges in a way that is informed by all that we know. Good decision making, then, is informed by information about what is going on outside of us, our primitive reaction to it in the form of physiological events interpreted as emotion, and analysis of the meaning of the situation performed by our more advanced frontal lobes. This complex process can only occur when the parts of our brain are communicating with one another.

The Impact of Strong Emotions

Recent studies of the brain have revealed the rapidity with which messages from the amygdala are transmitted to other areas of the brain and to sensory and motor systems, effectively blocking the connections that exist between other parts of the brain during normal, non-threatening conditions. The more intense the emotion, the greater the effect becomes of severing communication between the sensing part of the brain and the analytic processing part of our brain. In threat situations, all extraneous information is blocked, clearing the way for fast, dramatic, and effective response. This makes rational, consid-ered, objective thinking impossible, for good reason. In the time it would take to apply reason and judgment we might well be devoured by a saber toothed tiger!

Of course the situations we encounter in the workplace are rarely the sort that represent an immediate threat requiring a fight or flight response. These situations present a different sort of challenge. We may know intuitively that running away or expressing strong emotions to another with whom we have a difference is not going to help resolve the situation and is, in fact, much more likely to generate a similarly emotional and defensive response, starting a downward spiral of emotional exchanges. Knowing that this is counter-productive relative to our goal of finding a rational win-win solution doesn't always prevent us from acting emotionally.

It might seem best to simply suppress the emotion. However, in these situations, we need to be able to access information about what is going on around us and also to know what we think and *feel* about it. Being aware of what we are sensing, whether it feels like anger, fear, or just discomfort, is an important source of information. Certainly, we would not want to sacrifice our ability to know when something just doesn't feel right, even if we're not exactly sure why we feel that way. In fact, believing in one's intuition or "gut" is often strongly advised. But acting on those feelings alone, impulsively, is not likely to lead to the most desirable outcome. We need to be able to think about the situation in all of its dimensions in order to arrive at a plan of action that is most likely to lead to effective solutions and not damage relationships. We need to consider context, history, and a myriad of other relevant factors before responding. In short, we need to be able to transmit the instinctive, primitive sensory information to the more advanced processing part of our brain before reacting.

The key to making good choices regarding how we express emotions lies in lessening the intensity of the emotion in the moment to buy time for the processing to take place and enable a well-thought-out response, rather than one based only on primitive reaction to external stimuli. The less intense the emotion, the less it interferes with intra-brain communication and the less it has the power to impair rational thought.

Managing Our Own Emotions

Thankfully, we are capable of decreasing the intensity of emotions, though this is sometimes easier said than done. Even when the feelings are not intense, it can be difficult to put them aside long enough to objectively assess the situation. Often our impulse to act on emotions is powerful. Knowing how to postpone that uninformed reaction takes practice. Applying strategies like taking a deep breath, counting to ten, or stiffening some muscles that others cannot see works to buy time. If all else fails and emotions are taking over, one can find an excuse to leave the situation and schedule another time to continue the conversation.

Effectively managing our emotions requires becoming aware of what we are feeling and accepting it for what it is without judgment. Though it may seem paradoxical, self-acceptance is the first step to being able to put the feeling aside temporarily. Similarly, giving yourself permission to feel the way you do helps to lower the intensity of the feeling. There is considerable individual variance in how easy or difficult it is to do these things.

Self-Awareness, Acceptance, and Validation

Also referred to as mindfulness, self-awareness means being fully aware, in the moment, of what you are feeling. It is achieved by turning inward, tuning into body sensations, clearing the mind of extraneous thoughts, and being open to discovering what is true for you without any judgment. Whatever you discover, even things you may not have known about yourself or that you don't particularly like (e.g., I'm uncomfortable around certain kinds of people), does not have to be shared with anyone else. It will be useful only to you. Once you have gotten in touch with a feeling, it is helpful to put a name to it. This seems to help preserve knowledge of the feeling by making it more concrete and tangible. The more you are able to know your own feelings, the more you will ultimately be able to put them aside or even change them if you choose to. If you find that this is very difficult for you to do, you might consider practices such as yoga and meditation that can enhance this ability.

Another technique that can help increase the ability to recognize your emotions is to enlarge the vocabulary of words you have that describe feelings. For example, try finding a word that describes a feeling starting with every letter of the alphabet. Words that describe feelings are different than words that describe thoughts or physical sensations i.e. worried is a feeling, wishing for something is not. The more words to which you have ready access, the more likely you will be able to find a word that describes what you are feeling, leading to a more concrete experience of it and greater ability for your brain to process it.

Once the feeling is named, it is possible to simply accept it for what it is and give yourself permission to feel the way you do. For example, when someone does something that you experience as irresponsible, you might identify your feeling as disappointed and angry. As you think about the way you feel, you can also think about the larger context, the history of the situation and what you know about the other person. Given all of this, you may come to the conclusion that your feelings of disappointment and anger are entirely appropriate. Paradoxically, the more you think about this, the more the physical sensations associated with anger and disappointment dissipate. This allows you to think more clearly about what you would like the outcome of the situation to be and what actions you could take to make that happen. It also deters you from taking an immediate action or behaving in a way that may work against a good outcome. Your emotional response to the situation becomes just one piece of information to consider along with many others.

In fact, the feelings we have about the situation are relevant and should be known to others as part of the whole picture. Knowing that someone has felt frustrated, angry, satisfied, or saddened may contribute to the outcome. Talking *about* feelings can be a good and constructive thing. Again, it is *how* we talk about them that can determine whether or not they will be heard and understood as intended. Being able to talk about feelings without actively demonstrating them in tone of voice and gestures can be very helpful, though it may be difficult to do.

Managing Our Impact on Others

There are several things we can do to help others with whom we are engaged to manage their emotions as well. All of the same mechanisms which are working in us are working in them i.e. the instinctive response to fight or flee in the face of perceived threat or harm. Our goal is to help them resist the primitive urge to react by keeping the intensity of their emotions low and manageable.

Perhaps the most powerful thing we can do is simply to remain calm and unemotional ourselves. Conversely, when we approach someone in a way that conveys negative emotion toward them, whether in tone, gesture, body language, or words, we can be almost assured that their response will be similarly emotional. Once an emotional exchange has begun, it is extremely difficult to move it into a rational discussion. Even if the words we are saying are suggesting that there is a problem to be addressed, a calm and emotionally neutral demeanor helps the other person to hear and take in the meaning of the words.

Listening, Acknowledgment, and Validation

The more someone feels listened to, truly heard, validated and respected, the more they will be able to use their rational thought processes and not allow their behavior to be ruled by emotion. When people are given the opportunity to express their concerns, in a calm and rational way, they are more able to engage their higher-level reasoning capacity.

Understanding and validation are not the same as agreement. The person who has disappointed us may offer his or her reasons and explain all that has contributed to their behavior. A validating response would be to reflect back what they have said accurately and tell them you understand how they might see it that way. This would be followed by your view of the situation and your request for whatever you want to happen next, laying the groundwork for a rational exchange.

When exchanges like this occur, they are the basis for building trust and strengthening relationships. Over time, as conversations are dominated by authentic exchanges in which people are listening to one another to understand and to solve problems together, avoiding exchanges dominated by emotion, workplaces become healthier, more satisfying places to work.

Implications for Resolving Differences

At the core, resolving differences must be about assessing situations rationally, generating and assessing options and making well-thought-out decisions about solutions that achieve good long-term outcomes. The discussions that lead to such outcomes must first be focused on substantive issues and concerns, not emotional ones.

It is true that most differences have relational and emotional components, sometimes the product of past experiences, or simply because engaging with others around differences naturally awakens internal tension between wanting our preferred outcome, and our desire to keep relationships comfortable and easy. Others have suggested that these must be addressed first, before substantive issues can be discussed. While we agree that addressing these in a constructive way may help to create enduring solutions, we believe that this should occur only after substantive issues have been successfully addressed. Working together in the way we describe to resolve substantive issues builds trust and skills, and makes it far more likely that emotionally charged issues can be addressed constructively at a later time.

As we have shown in this chapter, we have the capacity for rational thought, even in situations that have emotional components. But our capacity for reason can be compromised when we allow our primitive instincts to dominate what is going on in our brain. The more we can lessen emotional intensity and strengthen the communication between primitive and more advanced parts of our brain, the better we are at rational thought and complex tasks such as solving organizational problems. Emotions are an important part or our human experience, but when we allow them to dictate behavior, we are less than our best.

We recognize that, within organizations, there are many people who are uncomfortable with any show of emotions (they may call this an outburst). There are others who will not feel heard or validated unless they have had an opportunity to express their feelings. The challenge of managing this divide can be met by addressing substantive issues first and by encouraging all to name their emotions and talk about them while minimizing the degree to which they are conveyed non-verbally.

Addressing substantive issues without first resolving emotional ones not only keeps us on track to find good solutions, it also helps to build stronger positive relationships and trust. When we work together in the best, most productive, respectful, and collaborative ways, we find that emotional issues often dissipate, resolve, or become irrelevant. Focusing on them first is far more likely to result in prolonged non-productive exchanges and lessened capability to do the hard work of understanding diverse views, generating creative options, and making good decisions.

Key Learning Points

- Because of the way our brains are structured, emotional reactions to external stimuli may not get transmitted to the regions of the brain that make decisions based on advanced processing, resulting in primitive instincts to fight or flee.

- These behaviors served us well in ancient settings where the threats were simple and called for a fight or flight response, but often lead us to behave inappropriately in settings like workplaces, where complex problems need to be resolved rationally.

- The more intense the emotion, the more it can interfere with intra-brain communication, higher-level decision making, and rational behavior.

- We have the capability to decrease the intensity of felt emotions by becoming self-aware, naming the feeling and accepting it without judgment. When this occurs, the emotion becomes just one of many pieces of information about the situation, allowing us to make a more nuanced and appropriate decision about how to respond.

- Sharing information about emotional and relational concerns can be very constructive when it is done without letting emotions be expressed non-verbally. We can help others do this by keeping non-verbal communication neutral and by listening, understanding, and validating what they have shared.

- In conflict situations, addressing substantive issues before emotional ones helps us to engage our rational brain and avoids the possibility of destructive exchanges, which can derail a constructive process. Addressing substantive issues in a calm, rational, respectful, and authentic manner not only leads to better solutions, it also helps to build trust and positive relationships. When people work together in this way, negative emotional concerns often dissipate or become irrelevant.

Chapter 4

The Power of Purpose:
Creating a Culture of Alignment

We have referred to "organizational culture" several times. We believe there is a powerful relationship between organizational culture and an organization's ability to effectively manage conflict. In order to maximize the power of that relationship, we will need to 1) define the concept of organizational culture in general; and 2) describe the attributes of culture that are most supportive of constructive conflict resolution practices.

A Definition of Organizational Culture

Imagine that a close friend or relative has just been hired by an organization and, because you know the organization intimately, has come to you for advice. You would proceed to tell the individual about the organization's values and how it operates. You would explain how people regard others in various jobs and levels, how people typically treat one another and, especially, what would likely get your friend in trouble and what would distinguish him or her. You would undoubtedly have many vivid stories to illustrate these and other aspects of how the organization lives its values—or how it doesn't. All of these attributes contribute to and define an organization's culture.

The culture of an organization is multi-layered, with *observable artifacts, practices, and behaviors* on the surface, *spoken values, beliefs, and ideologies* just beneath what is observable, and *unspoken beliefs and assumptions* at the base (Schein, 2006). Culture evolves over time as a product of what leaders and others do, what actions are taken with what results and what lasting lessons are learned. Often, the creation of culture is largely unintentional, though it may be examined intentionally and its appropriateness questioned when things are not going well. Ideally, organizations *do* become quite intentional about identifying the characteristics of a culture that are most likely to result in successfully implementing strategy. When they do, they systematically identify the practices and behaviors to be rewarded and reinforced and put policies in place that support them.

Figure 4.1: Two Ways to Think About Organizational Culture

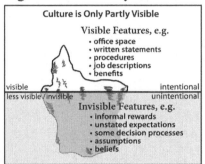

A Culture of Alignment

It is not unusual for an organization to espouse values and beliefs that are inconsistent with its real practices. The mission statements on the wall don't always line up with what happens day-to-day. Over time a conflicting set of unspoken values and beliefs replaces the spoken ones. When this is the case, the organizational culture is out of alignment with its stated values. The building blocks of tangible, real, on-the-ground culture are the actual practices; the way work "really gets done around here." The behavior that is actually rewarded or not rewarded and the spoken values that support and explain that behavior let people know what is expected of them. These expectations become the norms of the organization. When spoken values and intents are consistent with actual practices, the organization is said to be aligned.

Alignment is a necessary quality for organizations that want to become good at harnessing the positive power of differences. Organizations that are truly aligned have explicitly stated purpose, vision, strategies, goals, roles, practices, relationships, and a set of lived values and philosophies that are consistent with these statements.

We find that working through the Alignment Triangle (see Figure 4.2), top to bottom, helps organizations create strategies and establish priorities that keep everyone moving together in the same direction. This in itself minimizes much conflict. When differences do occur, having a common understanding of the organization's purpose gives people a common focus and objective.

Figure 4.2: Organizational Alignment

Relationships are at the bottom of the triangle not because they are unimportant, but because having shared understanding and agreement about substantive concerns—mission, goals, roles, and practices—often preempts many personal or emotional issues. As discussed in the previous chapter, focusing on rational and pragmatic concerns can help us be more effective in managing relationships.

Defining Mission or Purpose

Organizational alignment begins by defining a central purpose. While this may seem obvious, even trite, we are continually amazed at the number of organizations in which purpose is not universally shared or understood. We cannot overemphasize the importance of a clear, widely understood and agreed-upon mission or purpose for an organization. While we use the terms "mission" and "purpose" interchangeably, we actually think that "purpose" is a better word because its meaning is commonly shared. The purpose of any enterprise is its reason for being. It is its worth or value; what would be missing in the world if it did not exist.

Having a clear statement of purpose allows every person associated with the organization to feel that their work has meaning. It also underscores the fact that everyone is working toward the same end and that they are interdependent; no one person or function or department could achieve the purpose alone.

The extent to which shared purpose, strategy, and goals are defined, well articulated, and understood relates directly to individual's and group's ability to resolve differences. These shared objectives are the reason that it makes sense to subordinate one's own short-term benefit in favor of longer term organizational achievements.

A newspaper's statement of purpose as "to provide accurate and timely information to every segment of the community" creates the glue that unites people in coordinated activity. It gives people a reason to put aside short-term or entirely self-interested actions or priorities in favor of those that support the overarching purpose. It helps people lift themselves up out of petty motives to be willing to make small sacrifices for the whole.

It is not the statement on the wall that matters. It is the way the organization's purpose is understood and used by everyone to make decisions and direct behavior.

Vision, Strategy, and Goals

Similar to purpose, organizations that articulate a vision for the future, a strategy for moving toward it and specific goals for groups and individuals to relate to, create a powerful force for uniting people in mutually supportive activities. In particular, strategies and goals dictate priorities by creating a metaphorical North Star to indicate the correct path for going forward. Differing or competing priorities often underlie issues in conflicts that occur between departments or groups. When strategy and goals have been clearly defined (ideally, with input from all those responsible for carrying them out) and are clearly in support of (i.e. aligned with) purpose and vision, priorities can more easily be sorted out and agreed to.

Resource allocation, another major cause of conflict, generally follows from goals and priorities. Having these agreed to and aligned with purpose and vision makes it possible to resolve issues related to distribution of resources much more easily.

Roles

Another frequent cause of conflict is confusion over roles: "Who does what." A sign of strong management is a workforce that understands explicitly what each person, group, or department is responsible for. This is not to say that jobs are narrowly defined. In fact, the opposite is true. Each person is clear about what outcome, related to goals, priorities, strategies, he or she is ultimately responsible for and knows what must be done to achieve it. Defining roles in this way makes the need for interdependence obvious. "Give and take" becomes the norm.

Practices

By practices, we mean all the infrastructures that define how we operate. They include the rules, either written or unwritten, about how we make decisions, share information, assign tasks, manage and reward performance and so forth. Some organizations define many practices in formal ways, outlined in thick manuals; others rely on informal norms. In either case, as long as everyone understands and knows how to do what is needed to achieve the desired outcomes, it is useful to clearly define the organization's practices.

Relationships

Sometimes we help organizations sort out a personality clash among two or more employees. When that happens, we typically start by asking about clarity of goals, roles, and practices. In almost every case, when confusion about these is eliminated, the relationship issues are greatly diminished or go away all together.

We believe that co-workers only have to work with each other and achieve the outcomes they are tasked with; they don't have to like each other. The irony is that when they learn to work together to achieve a task, they often find that they *do* like each other because all of the petty reasons for their initial disagreements and mutual annoyances become much less important.

> *The software development department of a large company consisted of six teams of developers, each responsible for a distinct part of the development process. Each project, done for a particular internal client, was mapped out in a sequence of tasks that involved hand-offs from one team to another, all coordinated by a project integrator. Of course it was expected that each project would be completed on time and within budget. Each team was also responsible for routine tasks that were not directly related to the projects. As expected, the teams frequently clashed when one or another team caused a project to be delayed or to run over budget. Expecting the person in the integrator role to resolve these conflicts was generally ineffectual.*

With a neutral third party, the teams were helped to define their overall mutual goals, as well as each team's specific interest. They could then see where these overlapped or were in conflict, and what was getting in the way of a more collaborative approach to resolving their differences. Collectively, they came to understand and acknowledge that the way in which scarce resources (i.e. some individuals with specific, highly valued skills) were being hoarded was a significant cause of the problem. They also learned how to address their differences in a more direct and above-board way and to work out a process for deciding how to allocate resources when there were competing demands.

Norms and Values

Norms are the mechanisms by which culture tacitly conveys expectations. They are the unwritten rules that everyone knows must be adhered to in order to succeed. Values are also often not clearly communicated, though they underlie much of what actually happens. Both are keys to creating and sustaining a particular culture. While organizations vary tremendously, industry to industry, there are some norms and values that we believe are conducive to a culture that supports constructive resolution of differences across all sectors. Here are six of them.

All Individual Contributors are Valued

In some organizations there is much rhetoric around the sentiment "people are our most valued asset" that is not necessarily consistent with practices. Organizations that truly understand and believe that the success of the enterprise rests on enabling the success of every individual tend to behave in certain ways:

- Decisions are made with input from those who are affected and have relevant knowledge or information. Completely top-down decisions are the exception rather than the norm.

- Managers are expected to help their employees succeed and they are evaluated on that ability. Managers who are not good at enabling employee success (indicators might include high turnover, poor results on attitude surveys, many complaints) are themselves aided with training. If they cannot improve on this dimension, they themselves cannot succeed in the organization.

- Performance management systems are in place to help every employee understand what is expected of him or her. Feedback is given informally and frequently to allow each person to develop appropriately. There are no surprises and no guesswork.

- There is general understanding of what motivates individuals, e.g. feeling valued and important, having opportunities to use their skills, grow and be recognized for good work, a certain amount of autonomy and a great deal of respect.

- Individuals are respected for what they know and are allowed the autonomy to make decisions when appropriate. Managers are not necessarily the only ones to make decisions because individual contributors frequently have more detailed information about day-to-day events.

All Functions are Interdependent

Some organizations recognize inherently that they function as systems, with all parts interconnected, each impacting all the others. When this is the case:

- Starting at the executive level, all departments and functions are seen as equally important to the success of the organization, since no one part could get the job done without all the others. This attitude trickles down so that people at every level understand the need to work effectively with people in other departments.

- There are no "silos." Each department or function keeps the others informed of its activities and consults with those impacted by them. All departments work together in a coordinated fashion to move the organization toward its purpose.

- Individuals understand that there will be times when one department or function must make short-term sacrifices that serve the whole in the long run; rather than competing with one another, departments embrace the idea that in the long run everyone profits by the organization's success. ("A rising tide lifts all boats.")

> *In a publishing organization, the editorial department may see itself as most important to achieving the overarching purpose of providing news and information to the community. They also understand that they could not stay in business if the advertising department cannot generate enough revenue to cover expenses and make some profit for the owners and shareholders. They all understand and agree that, without the presses and the mail room, they could not deliver a product to their customers. They all are interdependent and the entire enterprise could not succeed without all of them working together in a coordinated way.*

Mistakes are Indicators of Problems to be Solved

Some organizations create a condition of perpetual fear by always needing a scapegoat for anything that goes wrong. This is unhealthy, not only for individuals but also for the organization, as it inhibits any kind of risk-taking, creativity or innovation. It also means that there is an orientation toward the past rather than the future.

Healthy organizations accept that most mistakes are not the result of individual neglect, intentional or not, but are related to systemic problems. They regard mistakes as indicators of something that needs to be done better and as an opportunity to learn. Recognizing that all employees want to succeed and that all perspectives are useful to understanding, they use mistakes as the basis for bringing people together to problem-solve with an orientation toward avoiding similar problems in the future and finding better ways to do things.

Diversity of Opinion and Viewpoint is Valued

Most people understand that no two human beings are exactly the same, yet many are surprised by the idea that, for any given situation, there is not just one truth. They are convinced that the way they see things is the way it is, not that it is the product of their own particular perspective. In fact, each person's perspective is the product of that person's "lens," which is drawn from their past experiences, their cognitive and emotional functioning, and all the things that make them unique.

Organizations that understand this reality also appreciate the value of bringing multiple perspectives to bear on any issue or problem to be solved. When many different points of view are considered, solutions are likely to be more creative, more holistic, and thoughtful. Though it may take longer to arrive at resolution and requires considerable skill, the superior outcome makes the time it takes to get to the solution worthwhile and, therefore, often easier to implement.

Organizations that value differences are also more likely to employ participative processes to solve problems, allowing people at all levels to be involved in thinking through important business issues. Involvement leads to buy-in, which leads to commitment.

Candor is a Good Thing

Candor is often confused with incivility. We are not endorsing rudeness or incivility. To be candid is to be straightforward, frank, and direct. One can be candid and still be tactful, rather than rude, taking the feelings and likely impact on the person being addressed into consideration when choosing how to phrase the message.

Being candid is, in fact, something you do *for* the other person and to strengthen the relationship. Most of us have been in situations in which someone harbors resentment or has negative thoughts about us or something we have done, but has not done us the service of letting us know. It doesn't feel good! Certainly, most people want to know what others are thinking and want the opportunity to clear up misperceptions, right wrongs and figure out ways to make the relationship work better in the future.

In organizations, the norm of not being candid causes all kinds of problems. Not only do individual relationships turn sour, whole groups or departments can become alienated and important issues left unaddressed and unresolved.

Resolving Differences is Everyone's Job

The idea that conflict and difference are a normal and necessary part of organizational life suggests that everyone ought to be able and be expected to handle the work of resolving differences. Managers may understand that they should not automatically resolve differences among those who report to them and may reasonably expect them to be capable of doing so themselves. If they do not have the skills, the manager might step in as facilitator, both to help them handle the current situation as well as develop skills for the future. Being able to resolve differences effectively becomes everyone's responsibility and part of their expected job performance.

It also suggests that other potential third parties, such as HR managers, push the task of resolving conflicts back to the employees involved or, alternatively, act as facilitators or mediators if necessary.

We have frequently seen HR managers get themselves into the role of "confidante" to an employee who unloads their complaints about another person and makes the HR person promise not to pass the information on. This becomes an unfortunate conflict-avoidance mechanism that renders the HR person ineffectual. We advise HR managers to tell the employee that they would like to help: They would be more than willing to help the person find the right words to have a productive conversation with the person with whom they have the issue, or to act as a neutral facilitator.

The Culture is the Foundation

In many organizations, culture is simply the unintentional by-product of what they do. In the best organizations, strategies for success are carefully thought out and detailed plans put in place to achieve them. In the best of the best, strategies include ideas about what kind of culture the organization needs to build in order to succeed.

Organizations that embrace all of the above are rare. Those that do are much farther along the road to creating environments in which differences are the fuel of positive, creative growth. But simply stating these principles doesn't get you there. They have to be lived and breathed every day. They have to be modeled by people of influence and they have to be backed up with policies and practices that promote them. There have to be rewards for people who live up to them and consequences for those who don't.

This foundation lets people know that, to succeed in their organization, they have to possess and practice the skills necessary for managing differences constructively. While never perfect, organizations that hold and live by these beliefs find a way to convey them, as in the situation below.

Procter & Gamble's largest manufacturing facility manufactures multiple consumer paper products 24/7. During the lengthy startup of this facility, operating practices and procedures were defined very precisely because any downtime in the highly complex pulp and paper making operations would incur huge costs. Pulp making and paper making were physically separated by approximately 100 yards and housed in separate buildings. Technicians who operated these two parts of the facility would not naturally see or work directly with one another. Quality of pulp is closely monitored both as it leaves the pulp mill and when it enters the paper mill. Both parts of the operation run similar tests on the pulp. When the paper mill technicians determine that the pulp is not of satisfactory quality, they can shut down the system, causing considerable difficulty for the pulp mill whose storage capacity is limited. It was not unusual for the quality tests performed at each location to not agree.

When this happened, the technicians would typically take the issue to their respective managers who would debate the testing practices and institute even more rigorous testing processes. The pulp and paper mill operators would wait for management to dictate the revised testing practices and decisions.

After many frustrating occasions, the management of the pulp and paper mill operations decided to create a cross-training program involving both departments. Operators involved in conducting quality tests and in operating equipment would spend time in each other's area to become trained on the others' practices and processes. The operators, who by this time saw one another as "the enemy," resisted strongly. Nevertheless, they were asked to rotate through a training assignment in each others' areas and were given little direction about what they should learn. This rotation continued for six months, with operators spending a week at a time in each others' area.

As time went on, the quality tests became more and more consistent and the occurrences of pulp mill shut down became fewer. Instead of operators not communicating with one another when an aberrant test could be anticipated, they began walking to one another's work area and taking breaks together. They had gotten to know one another on a personal basis as a result of the exchange program and they now saw one another as individuals with similar challenges within their operating areas of responsibility.

There had always been a set of general principles which were intended to guide the practices across this huge manufacturing facility. These principles included things like: "Do What's Right"—"Pass the Word"—"Always Serve the Customer" etc. While these may seem a bit general and high-level, the pulp and paper mill operators began to behave in a spirit that represented these guidelines. Eventually, the operators were the ones who created new operating standards for testing and identifying additional ways of working together across this organizational boundary.

Key Learning Points

- Organizations can consciously and intentionally create the culture they believe is needed. A thoughtful, values-based, deliberately implemented organizational culture can facilitate working through differences effectively.

- Clarity and consistency of purpose, practices, and values creates organizational alignment. Aligned organizations are able to consistently support the values they espouse, which can include those that enable constructive use of differences.

- When individual contributors are respected for their knowledge and expertise, and enabled to make decisions, they are also more likely to take responsibility for working through differences constructively.

- Organizations that value and reward directness, diversity of opinion, and problem-solving processes over a "one right answer" mentality have an advantage. When individuals are rewarded for digging in their heels and insisting that their way is the only way, others get the message that this is the way to "win" in this organization.

- When everyone is rewarded for working together in a cooperative, collaborative way the results tend to be better solutions and successful outcomes that benefit the organization as a whole as well as the individuals who are a part of it.

A Practical Process for Resolving Differences Constructively

"If I had an hour to solve a problem, I'd spend 55 minutes thinking about the problem and 5 minutes thinking about the solution."—Attributed to Albert Einstein

"We must love them both—those whose opinions we share, and those whose opinions we reject. For both have labored in the search for truth and both have helped us in the finding of it."—St Thomas Aquinas

Conflict in any context is rarely simple or one-dimensional. Even a seemingly superficial difference has, at the very least, some factual and historical data as well as the human elements of motivation, desire, thoughts, beliefs, emotions, and behaviors of the people involved. Add the backdrop of an organization, with its own rich cultural texture, and you have a veritable stew of elements that may appear impossible to deal with at all, let alone in a constructive way. It is little wonder that many people still allow themselves to be taken over by their primitive "fight or flight" instincts when they encounter differences.

As we will learn, "fight or flight", while not always a *de*structive response, is not often the most *con*structive response. We tend to employ primitive, instinctive responses when we are unaware of alternatives or lack the skills and abilities to successfully apply them. The antidote is to learn and practice a set of processes, tools, and skills that enable us to make a conscious decision about how to approach a particular situation.

Slowing down the whole process is a key part of keeping it constructive. Rather than being in reactive automatic response mode when one encounters a difference, our model requires a thoughtful five-step process: ***Prepare, Engage, Diverge, Create, Agree & Implement.***

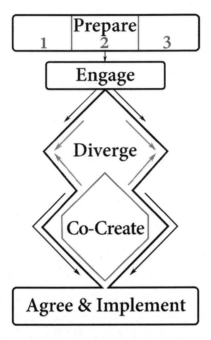

In some instances, these may all take place in a short time span of one or two meetings, or they may extend over several days, weeks or even months, depending on the complexity of the issues and the degree of differences between the parties. Though the five steps may sometimes overlap or blur, we believe that each of them must take place to produce the best outcomes.

Though we present the steps as discreet and the process as linear, we know that in real life things are typically much messier than this implies. While the chronology we present is idealized, we believe that as long as the principles are applied, good outcomes can be achieved.

As discussed in Chapter 2, truly constructive resolutions to organizational issues do not just make them go away temporarily. They are solutions that address root causes, resolve the issues in ways that not only satisfy the parties, leaving them feeling like respected and valuable contributors, but benefit the entire organization as they take the long view. Solutions such as these strengthen relationships rather than leaving them frayed, and create new pathways for innovative thought.

Collaborative, win-win solutions may not be possible or even appropriate in every instance of organizational conflict. Certainly, there are times when "going to the mat" for what you believe is the best outcome is justified, just as it may be wisest, in some situations, to accommodate another's wishes or even to avoid directly addressing the issue. This is true because it almost always takes more time to try to reach the best, mutually acceptable solution than it does to settle for an expedient compromise, to accommodate or just avoid. Therefore, it may not be appropriate when the issues are not important or there is too much time urgency.

There are, however many reasons to apply collaborative win-win techniques and approaches in many instances of organizational conflict. The most compelling reason is that the organization as a whole stands to benefit when individuals and groups take the long and broad view rather than basing their actions on narrow, short-term interests. Collaborative approaches typically result in better, more effective and creative solutions, contributing to the organization's success. Because the success and viability of the organization are ultimately in everyone's best interests as long as they remain with the organization, individuals ultimately benefit even when they must make short-term sacrifices. Individuals applying these principles also benefit by enhancing their reputations as effective leaders dedicated to ends larger than their own narrow self-interest. In addition, working relationships are strengthened over time, morale is lifted and norms that reward constructive, collaborative processes are created, all contributing to a positive culture and successful organizational outcomes.

In this section, we will outline the specific skills needed to carry out the ***Prepare, Engage, Diverge, Co-Create, Agree & Implement*** strategy. A general rule is that the more care and effort are put into the earlier steps, the easier the later steps become. We have devoted three chapters to the first step: ***Prepare.***

Chapter 5

Prepare—Part One: Understand the Situation

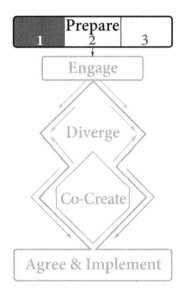

Preparing to resolve a difference involves taking an objective step back from the situation to gather information, apply analytical tools and make some decisions. The first part of preparation is directed at fully understanding and analyzing the elements of the situation; What's going on here? What are the factors underlying the situation? Why has it not been resolved? The second part is a bit more personal; it involves gathering information about and applying analytical tools to the thoughts, emotions and behaviors of those involved, including yourself.

We are framing this discussion under the assumption that the reader is a participant in the situation rather than a third party, e.g. a manager whose employees are involved, a human resource manager, or a consultant. We have made this choice because we think it is the most challenging perspective. If it is the case that the reader is acting as a facilitator or mediator to help others resolve the situation, the Preparation phase would include gathering information through observation and informal interviews. The purpose remains the same: to gain as much understanding as possible without making judgments.

Becoming an Objective Observer

The more complex the situation, the more important it is to be able to "take the view from the balcony" to observe the entire situation in an unbiased way. We all have a tendency to see what is going on from our own vantage point, without acknowledging that it may look very different if we were standing at another angle or from someone else's vantage point. To use another metaphor, if we're down in the cornfield, we can only see the row that we are in. We miss seeing the whole cornfield and therefore miss a great deal of information—how large it is, which parts are growing faster, where there might be a blight—unless we can get above it. As long as we're in our own row, we may actually have a very inaccurate picture of what is going on. In fact, we may be convinced that what we see is the whole "truth" rather than realizing it is only our own "truth" and wrongly judge someone else who sees it differently.

We recognize that becoming an objective observer of a conflict in which you are directly involved may be easier said than done. It is, however, an essential first step. Perhaps it would be more accurate to say that the essential first step is recognizing the need to adopt the role of objective observer during this preparatory stage. That in itself is an accomplishment, as it requires putting one's emotions on hold.

Some people have a more difficult time than others putting aside their emotions long enough to become an objective observer. (See Chapter 3 for a more detailed discussion.)

Here are some suggestions:

- Recognize that there is almost always more than one legitimate viewpoint for any situation. The goal is not to prove that you are "right" but to understand the whole of what has contributed to the differences.

- Remind yourself that your emotions are a legitimate and valuable part of who you are and there is no fault or shame in feeling whatever it is you feel. In fact, being aware of your feelings will be an important part of the process of re-solving the difference. However, for this part of the process it is important to put them aside temporarily.

- Get very clear about what you are feeling—not why, but what. Name the feelings so that you can almost picture them as objects. Imagine that you can actually take your emotions and place them in a box or a drawer where they are still accessible to you but are not interfering with your ability to think rationally. Use this or some other imagery to take control of how you manage your emotions.

- If this is something that continues to be difficult for you, we recommend a practice such as yoga or some other form of reflective exercise that involves breathing and relaxation.

Gathering Information

Once in a frame of mind to observe objectively, you can begin to gather information about the nature of the conflict, what may be contributing to it, and keeping it from becoming resolved. There are many areas to pursue.

Facts

In any situation there are some facts that can be considered "givens," though not everyone will necessarily agree on what is uncontestable fact and what isn't. Part of the background of a conflict might actually be a difference of opinion regarding what can be taken as fact and what is the best source of a par-ticular kind of information. Be very careful to distinguish facts, i.e. verifiable information, from opinion.

*In our work with a magazine editor, she was unswervingly
emphatic about the fact that her staff had accomplished
more in the last year with fewer members than the year
before. Her boss and the CFO disputed her numbers. It
was not until the person working for the CFO, who had
actually compiled the information for his boss, compared
his assumptions and process with those of the editor that
everyone could understand the source of the discrepancy.
Once the facts were cleared up and agreed upon, a more
rational process could take place.*

In this situation it was reasonably easy for everyone to agree
on what constituted fact. In others, there can be a significant
amount of disagreement about what is fact:

*The manager of customer relations and his counterpart
in advertising sales disagreed about the level of satisfaction customers experienced with regard to a particular
product. The first was relying on anecdotal reports from
his staff, who had many stories to tell about dissatisfied
customers. The ad sales manager had data from a survey
done by another department that reported a high level
of customer satisfaction. Both believed their information
was more valid than the other person's. Before either set
of facts could be accepted as true and meaningful, more
investigation had to be done.*

In this case, information in the form of anecdotes and reports un-
deniably exists, but does not necessarily show the facts. Present-
ing original documents and interview data can be helpful. Often
it is best to gather primary information yourself if time permits.

In some situations there can be an enormous amount of information to consider. While it may not be necessary to gather
an exhaustive amount of information at this stage, we suggest
that it is a very good idea to at least be aware of what kinds
of information are pertinent to the issues at hand and to have
some idea of what sources exist for each so that more can be
retrieved with relative ease if needed.

Processes, Practices, Structures

Organizations accomplish their work by applying processes, sometimes very intentionally and sometimes in a relatively automatic way. The kinds of processes and practices that most often contribute to conflict are ones that directly impact people's sense of competence and feelings about how they are regarded and treated by others, e.g. how information is or is not shared; how decisions are made; whether or not they have opportunities to express their ideas or concerns. Structures include the way people are arranged relative to functions, tasks, and one another. For example, organizations can be highly centralized or decentralized, hierarchical or flat; functions can be very discreet from one another or highly interconnected; people can be arranged in permanent functional roles or they may be "matrixed" into flexible project teams. These differences have a direct impact on information sharing and communication, the nature of relationships, and how decisions are made.

> A group of software developers made up of multiple teams is collectively responsible for developing and delivering software to the production department. Each team works on multiple projects and works relatively independently of one another despite the fact that each of their products must get integrated into a whole before it can be delivered. The delivery manager oversees product integration and is the liaison to the internal client. There are rarely opportunities for all of the teams to come together to plan a project time-line, to learn what projects each team is working on, or what other challenges they are facing. When delivery dates are missed, there is a tendency among the team leaders to blame one another or the delivery manager because they are largely unaware of what each team is doing.

In this case, there are several process and structural elements that may be contributing to ongoing conflict, e.g. lack of role clarity and authority of the delivery manager to make decisions about schedules and time-lines; lack of information sharing among team leaders; issues about how staffing allocations are made and resources shared. In complex situations like this, it is essential to "take the view from the balcony" to observe the whole as objectively as possible and to understand all of the relevant processes, practices, and structures.

Goals, Objectives, Priorities

Most organizations do a reasonably good job of stating goals and objectives yet often fall short of making priorities clear. Is the primary overarching goal to make a profit, to serve customers well, to produce a quality product, to satisfy the board or stockholders, to serve some greater good? Are we more concerned about volume of sales or profit margins? Does the goal of meeting a deadline ever overrule quality? What about safety? Ask about what are the primary goals in most organizations and the answer you will most likely get is "All of them." Fine … but on-the-ground, day-to-day decisions about what to do first, how much time to devote, how to staff and allocate resources, etc. flow from choices about priorities.

While no one may be willing to admit that meeting a deadline is sometimes more important than quality or even safety, we all may tacitly understand that there are times when we are expected to behave as if that were the case. Perhaps that is the common perception, but it is not actually consistent with management philosophy. When, if ever, are we justified in denying service to a potential customer or client? When does the need to fix an immediate problem take precedence over working on a very high priority but longer term project? When is overtime justified?

In a sense, these choices can be thought of both as representing the *interests* of the organization and a reflection of the *values and beliefs* of the organization. Ideally, these are all consistent, though often this is not the case. To the extent that they are muddled, inconsistent, unclear priorities can be a source of conflict. For every complex question of this nature that arises, the potential for conflict is there. What can we learn about competing priorities and the circumstances that contribute to them?

Our software developers were faced with several compet-
ing priorities: the need to serve the internal client (the
Production Department) both by being instantly avail-
able to fix real-time production problems and to work on
the highest priority new product developments; to keep
up with backlogged projects; to make sure that each
new software product did what it was supposed to do;
to coordinate with all the other teams so the products
could be integrated to meet the project deadline; to keep
their own staff productive without excessive overtime;
and so on. Each team and team leader had to make de-
cisions every day about what would be attended to first.
As long as they made these decisions independently of
one another, there were bound to be conflicts among the
teams and with the delivery manager responsible for fa-
cilitating integration and product delivery.

History of This Situation:
Behaviors, Feelings, and Relationships

This factor relates to the specifics of the particular situation that has created a conflict or difference, including the nature of the relationship among protagonists and their individual feelings, thoughts, and behaviors regarding one another and the situation.

Every relationship has its own history. How well do the people know one another? Has the relationship been collegial, competitive, aloof, warm, distrusting? What has happened to shape the relationship? To what degree are the roles interdependent? In what way? How have they worked together and with what outcomes?

Each person also has his or her own set of feelings and thoughts about the others and about the situation itself. What emotions are involved? Are people angry, sad, fearful, suspicious, hurt, or humiliated? Are any of these feelings intensely felt or are they mild? When were these feelings first experienced, and what may have triggered them? How are people thinking about the situation? Do they think they have been disrespected? Do they believe they are owed an apology? Does anyone believe the issue is purely professional or entirely personal? Do they each vehemently believe they are right and that there can be only one "right"?

What has each person actually done leading up to the difference? How has each contributed to the current situation? What have they done to try to resolve it? How have their behaviors impacted the relationship? How have other people been impacted and how does that affect the situation?

By gathering information about the situation, you have done more than is immediately apparent. In the process, you have most likely become a far more objective observer than you were when you began. You have raised yourself up "into the balcony" and "above the cornfield" and can see the situation in its entirety, rather than from the limited vantage point with which you started. You are ready to apply some tools to make sense of what you know and further prepare for the process of engagement.

In contrast to the concrete information you've gathered so far, there are other, more conceptual and theoretical kinds of information that can further inform your understanding and aid in preparation. These include theories about what motivates people to want what they want and ideas about how organizational values and culture influence peoples' behavior.

Interests, Needs, Motivations

There is some controversy regarding definitions of interests, needs, wants, motivations, etc. among behavioral scientists and specifically among those of us investigating conflict. While we could easily fill another book with that discussion, we will say simply that, for our purposes, we are lumping all of these terms into one category. What we are talking about is whatever it is that the protagonists in a conflict situation care about most.

We can also make some generalizations about what is most important to most people in the context of their work life. As in Abraham Maslow's *Hierarchy of Needs*, the needs or interests that are in the forefront for a person may vary at different times and for different situations, depending on the person's ability to satisfy the most basic of those needs. We believe the vast majority of people in organizations are motivated to survive, thrive and, ultimately succeed in their work life. And, as in Maslow's hierarchy, which of these is prominent at a given time depends on many factors.

Figure 5.1: Maslow's Hierarchy of Needs
Adapted from Maslow, 1954

At the most basic level is physical safety. In the workplace, this can relate to working conditions and basic levels of pay that allow a person to provide shelter, food, etc. for themselves and their family. People who work in very dangerous jobs, like miners, are probably much more concerned about physical safety than other needs, though when those needs are satisfied, they are more able to focus on higher-order interests.

Closely related to physical safety is the need for psychological safety. This is particularly relevant to the workplace, where it can be satisfied or threatened in many ways, e.g. knowing or not knowing what is expected, getting or not getting feedback about performance, knowing it is or is not possible or likely to be successful at a task or job. The need for psychological safety can become the predominant interest for individuals in an environment in which they are subjected to humiliation or punishment.

The next need or interest has to do with the desire to thrive, or simply the desire to do well. It is closely related to a person's identity as someone who feels positively about his or her ability to contribute and is perceived that way by others. It can take the form of being accepted and/or respected by others, demonstrated by recognition, praise, or appreciation for one's contribution. Being made to feel different or not an accepted part of the group may bring this need into the foreground for anyone.

Individuals have their own expectations for themselves with regard to what represents achievement and success. For some people, professional accomplishments are the main source of their sense of identity and self-respect; this may be less true for others. This can vary considerably depending on the stage of life a person is in and other highly variable personal circumstances. In the workplace, a certain level of autonomy and opportunity for challenging job assignments, growth and development can be tied to self-respect or self-esteem. Being "micro-managed" or being deprived of opportunities to advance are examples of circumstances that might lead someone to be most concerned with interests related to self-esteem. Issues with others outside the workplace can also contribute to a loss of self-esteem and move someone to be more focused on this than on success.

Once someone is no longer concerned with survival and is secure in their identity as positive contributors, they can focus on the motivation to succeed, which can also take several forms. In our culture, it is not unusual for people to measure their success by outward indicators, e.g. title, pay, number of people managed. Many people also have internal measures of success that have to do with their own goals, ambitions, values, and passions.

This discussion would not be complete without a reference to power. While we do not consider power, in the sense of power over other people, to be a legitimate need or motivation, we cannot ignore the fact that the acquisition of power is a prominent interest for many people in organizations. Power can be represented by such things as the number of people reporting to someone, the amount of resources one controls, office size or location, or the amount of money they earn. Power can also be the ability to influence others to get something done or to achieve particular outcomes. When the interest is the acquisition of power in the service of achieving outcomes that are of benefit to the organization, it can be a positive expression of success motivation. When power is seen as an end rather than a means to something of benefit for the larger good, it may be quite destructive. However, power, like other motivators, is neither good nor bad in and of itself. It must be understood as an interest and considered as an element in a conflict situation.

In an assessment of motivation, whether our own or others, it is important to be dispassionate and non-judgmental. The benefit is in understanding what makes that person tick. What is important to him or her? The more we can understand this element, the better equipped we will be to negotiate.

Several team leaders for the software development teams expressed their interests this way: "We don't want to be the team responsible for making a mistake. We want to get it right so we work on our part of the project up until the last minute. We also have to juggle our staff to meet various project deadlines, so we are not so willing to let other teams know who is working on what because they might request someone who is not busy at the moment but we know will be the best person for a job that is coming up. No one else knows exactly what we are working on or what our priorities are; if they did, we would have less control over how we staff and how we schedule work."

These people's interests were largely concerned with success and the power to control their own resources in the service of accomplishing their work effectively. This is an example of a very common organizational dilemma: Everyone wants to be successful and to "get it right" but there are other elements in the system that make it difficult for one group to succeed without it being at the expense of another group. This, in turn, creates a less than optimal outcome for the organization. However, this example serves to illustrate power being used to further goals that will ultimately benefit the organization as a whole.

Understanding the interests of everyone involved is an extremely important step to becoming prepared for a productive engagement. While it is not always possible to discover other people's true interests, it is always useful to gather as much information as possible and attempt to understand what is truly important to them. We must offer a cautionary note regarding the tendency to fill in the blanks with unchecked assumptions or to apply judgments to what we believe to be other's interests. As in all of this investigatory activity, objectivity is required. It may be that the best we can do in understanding the motivations of others is to assemble what factual information we have about them, juxtapose that with whatever else we know about the situation and about human nature, and come to some tentative hypotheses.

Values and Beliefs

All organizations have underlying values and beliefs that guide what they do. Some organizations state their values clearly and make a real attempt to act consistently with them. Others may not state values clearly or at all; some may be unaware of them; others may state them but act inconsistently. Values and beliefs can relate to many things: what it means to be successful; what it *takes* to be successful; what we owe our customers; how we regard our competitors; what responsibility we have to other stakeholders; how we treat one another; how decisions should be made etc. Sometimes, different parts of an organization have values and beliefs that are quite distinct from other parts, or there are competing values even within a group or department. Having a clear understanding of the values that lie at the core of people's behavior is extremely helpful in sorting through a conflict situation.

> *In the world of newspaper publishing, it is generally the case that the editorial side of the organization has very strong values regarding how one goes about reporting the news. A frequently held belief is that there should never be any relationship between whether and how a story is reported and who buys advertising in the paper. Editors tend to believe that the fundamental purpose of the newspaper is to report the truth in as unbiased a way as possible and that allowing information about advertisers to influence them in any way would be counter to that value. As a result, they may believe that ad sales staff are not welcome in the newsroom and there should be minimal, if any, contact between sales representatives and reporters. Advertising departments, believing that revenues from advertising are of primary importance to keep the paper viable (not to mention keeping their commissions healthy), value a closer relationship between the two functions and generally believe that it can sometimes be appropriate to give more coverage to stories of interest to advertisers. They generally believe that there should be a more open line of communication between the two departments and greater acknowledgment of the interdependence of the two functions.*

When such divergent values exist within an organization, many other kinds of disagreements may result. The difference might seem to be about something as concrete as who should attend a particular meeting or how a role should be assigned, when at its core, it is the deeply held value that is the cause. This can add to the difficulty of resolving even seemingly trivial differences.

Organizational Culture

Several of the categories already discussed, most notably "processes, practices, and structures" and "values and beliefs" have considerable overlap with descriptions of the culture of the organization you are investigating. In addition to the definition of organizational culture provided in Chapter 4, we suggest that cultural attributes can most easily be detected by asking questions like "What does it take to succeed in this organization?", "How does work really get done in this place?", and "What gets rewarded and what gets punished here?" In this way, we can understand the often unspoken norms that dictate behavior. It is sometimes the case that norms operate quite distinctly from those that are articulated. The most visible expressions of culture, including such things as how people dress, the physical space, furniture and décor, are really superficial artifacts of the culture. You must look deeper to fully understand what is really guiding behavior:

> One organization we know of outwardly places great value on having issues out on the table and people being candid and open with one another; in practice, there is much secrecy and many topics that are taboo. In another organization the same value is stated and, in fact, people are typically very good at being direct with one another, problems are not allowed to go unaddressed and people are quite skilful at communicating.

> At a third organization, there is tremendous pressure to "do things right the first time," and the message that "failure is not an option" is stated loudly and clearly. While the intent is to instill a level of quality, precision, and accountability, in practice, it has produced a culture in which people are punished for mistakes. As a result, people behave cautiously and have a tendency to blame one another for things that go wrong rather than trying to identify the source of errors and correct them.

These are relatively simplistic illustrations of cultural attributes. To gather information about the culture of your organization, we recommend that you intentionally observe how things work for a few days, using an objective and impartial perspective rather than seeing things from the slightly biased perspective of someone inside the organization. Use the kind of questions we noted above, make notes as you go and generate a list of cultural attributes. Note how consistent the messages are with the reality of what goes on and how much widespread understanding there is of the actual culture. The less clarity and consistency, the more difficult it may be to resolve differences.

Key Learning Points

- Placing yourself in the role of investigator allows you to become a more objective observer of the situation. This emotional distancing is extremely helpful in all phases of working to resolve the issue constructively.

- Gathering information about all aspects of the situation helps you think about and plan the best way to approach seeking resolution.

- Information gathering can include information about the organization that is relevant to the situation, for example:

  - Facts and data that are verifiable;

  - Processes and practices typically employed to get work done in the organization;

  - Goals and priorities related to outcomes valued by the organization;

  - Things that have happened in the past that relate to the situation.

- Information can also be gathered that is less concrete and more theoretical, that can help you to better understand the situation from a more objective perspective, for example:

- The common themes and theories about how people experience needs, interests and motivations;

- How organizational values, beliefs, and culture influence and shape the behavior of people who work in them.

Skill Building Activities

For Everyone	For Managers & Leaders
Practice "taking the view from the balcony": think about an actual meeting and imagine you are looking down at it from above, where no one can see you.	Think about how current organizational norms and expressed values support or discourage collaborative problem solving. What can you do to encourage and reward collaboration?
• What do you see? Describe the activity without making judgments	
• What interpersonal dynamics do you observe?	Allow time for people to gather information before rushing to conclusions. Expect them to be prepared and informed.
• Is the topic being discussed in a constructive way? Are people listening to one another?	
• Do they seem to be concerned about what is good for the organization?	
How is this view different from the way you saw the meeting as a participant?	
If you could have this meeting over again, how might you participate differently?	
Share these observations with another trusted colleague who was also in the meeting. Do they see it similarly or differently?	

Chapter 6

Prepare—Part Two:
Analyze the Information for Clues

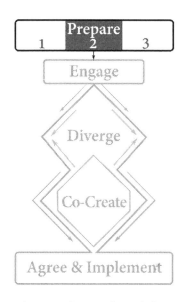

All of the information you've gathered forms the background of the current situation and is helpful to the degree that it can be viewed collectively and analyzed in a way that provides clues for how to proceed. We suggest three analytical tools or lenses that can be useful. The first is Force Field Analysis, which can be helpful in arranging the information to suggest a strategy. The second, Integrative Assessment, looks at the array of information to determine the degree to which a truly integrative ("win-win") solution is possible and the third, Level Analysis, considers the sources of the difference as clues to determine where to focus solution-seeking processes.

As the word "analytical" suggests, this is a rational, dispassionate way of relating to the situation. It will not appeal to everyone, particularly people who tend to view interpersonal differences primarily through the lens of emotions. We believe that this rational view is of value, perhaps even more so for people who do not naturally approach situations in this way. As we suggested in the last chapter, the process of gathering information has most likely already increased your ability to think more objectively about the situation. The tools given here can be used again, later in the process, when more information has emerged and as a way to build collective insights.

Force Field Analysis

Force Field Analysis allows us to view the current situation in its entirety as a system or network of countervailing forces. The first step in using this tool is to describe the situation in terms of a temporary state that is somewhere between the current state and the desired state. For example, the software development team we described in Chapter 4 needed the capacity to *effectively and efficiently integrate each component into the product required by the customer and deliver it on time*. This is a way to describe the future desired outcome rather than describing "the problem," Another way to think about this statement is that it describes the situation in a positive, or *appreciative*, rather than a negative, way. As we will see, thinking about the situation in this way will prove valuable in later stages of the process.

The next step is to consider all of the positive and negative forces that are contributing to the situation as described in this statement. Forces that are pushing the problem toward resolution are thought of as *driving forces*. For example, in the case of the software engineers, "intense pressure to deliver products on time" is a driving force, pushing people to want to solve the problem. Note that this, in itself, may not be thought of as a good thing. It is "good" only in that it tends to make people want to address and resolve the problem. Forces that are creating obstacles to resolution are considered *restraining forces*, e.g. "there is not one overarching goal for the team as a whole" makes it less likely that solving the problem is a high enough priority for people to take the time to address it. (See Table 6.1.) There are some forces that will turn up on both sides, because some things, such as the extreme time demands and time urgency of some kinds of projects, can have both a driving and restraining effect on the issue at hand.

Once arrayed, the information can be subjected to several inquiries:

- Which driving forces, if increased, and which restraining forces, if decreased, would have the greatest impact?
- Which of these forces are most amenable to change?

Which Forces Have the Greatest Impact?

Analysis will be based on some educated guessing, which is best done by those most knowledgeable about the entire situation. Consider which factors could have the greatest impact on resolving the issue at hand in the most complete and enduring way, and in a way that preserves or improves future relationships.

Going back to the software developers from the previous chapter, and looking at the list of forces, several stand out as potentially significant in their ability to impact the situation:

- Performance-related reward system for the individual, not the group
- No overarching goal
- Lack of clear priorities
- Delivery manager role unclear, not well performed
- Each team unaware of others' backlog of work
- Scarce resources leading to hoarding
- "Blame" culture
- Discomfort with angry feelings
- Avoidance behaviors of team leaders

Which Forces are Most Amenable to Change?

There are always some things that are relatively amenable to change by the people directly involved and some that are not. Often, there are large organizational-culture issues that require sustained actions at multiple levels of the organization. Though these may be most beneficial in the long term, they are not going to improve the immediate situation. There also may be personal, individual feelings and behavioral preferences that may or may not be amenable to change, depending on how long, how deeply, and how intensely they are held.

In this case, of the items that potentially have the greatest impact (see the list above) there are several forces that are probably out of the direct control of the people involved, e.g. reward systems, scarce resources, and culture. However, the structural forces, goals, priorities, and role clarity are amenable to change by this group, as is their lack of communication about backlogged work. Also, because of the warm personal relationships among these people, it is quite likely that their anger can be resolved. Modifying avoidance behaviors may also be possible, though more difficult.

The greatest value of the Force Field tool is its ability to display the situation as a system of factors that influence one another, rather than as dichotomous or polarized points of view. When all the participants in a conflict situation can see this together, it can be a powerful way to move people toward seeing the potential for a comprehensive, collaborative solution. We recommend using it not only in this preparatory stage, but also in the first step of the engaged, resolution-seeking work.

Table 6.1: Driving and Restraining Forces Affecting On-time Delivery

Driving Forces	Restraining Forces
High achievement drive of software developers; personal pride in strong record of performance	No one overarching goal for the team as a whole; each team has its own goals
Technical skill of software developers	Extreme time demands on everyone
Importance of high-quality software products to the company	Lack of clear priorities; competing priorities among different projects
Intense pressure to deliver products on time, especially when related to operating system	Unwillingness or inability of delivery manager to resolve differences among teams; lack of clarity of delivery manager role and authority to make and enforce decisions
Manager wants team leaders to be able to resolve their differences without involving him	The majority of team leaders prefer to avoid dealing with differences directly
Many team leaders have personal relationships outside the workplace	Performance-related reward system for individual performance (not group)
Team leaders have high personal regard for one another	Organizational culture includes a tendency to blame and punish people for mistakes
Organization places highest value on uninterrupted service to external customers	Sense of urgency about products that relate to immediate production problems
Few recent high profile late product deliveries	Each team has own backlog of project work; teams are not aware of each others' workload
Discomfort with recently expressed anger among otherwise respectful colleagues	Shared human resources across teams due to scarcity; some resource hoarding

Integrative Assessment

The Dictionary of Conflict Resolution defines "integrative" as "a condition in which disputants can achieve joint gain or satisfy their respective interests without significant loss." The opposite of an integrative solution is a "distributed" one, defined as "a condition in which there are few or no possibilities for joint gain in the resolution of a dispute or in which the satisfaction of one party's interests is at the direct expense of another party's interest, thereby requiring a division or distribution of a contested resource."

In any situation involving a difference it is possible for there to be potential for a completely integrative solution, a completely distributed solution, or some combination of the two. Given that the goals of resolving differences in organizations include satisfying all parties, strengthening relationships among those who must continue to work together, and creating enduring high-quality solutions that benefit the organization, it is clear that the more integrative the solution the more beneficial it will be.

While not every situation has the potential for an entirely integrative solution, the degree to which it is possible relates directly to the strength of shared, overarching purpose and common interests. Whether or not it is clearly stated, entities within an organization always possess a common interest in the continuing viability of the whole organization, its continued success, and ability to achieve its mission and goals. Therefore, there is always a reasonably high potential for an integrative solution to issues that occur among members of an organization.

In judging the potential for an integrative solution, it is also helpful to consider the degree to which there are overlapping or complementary interests. Overlapping interests are those that can be satisfied with the same solution because all parties want the same thing and it is not a scarce resource—there is enough for everyone. Complementary interests can also be satisfied with the same solution but for a different reason—there is the ability to exchange something that one party wants and the other has and doesn't need, or there is one solution that satisfies different interests.

In examining the list of forces for the software developers, we can identify the following items that could contribute to an integrative solution:

- Many shared purposes and goals, e.g. contribute to outcomes that are valued by the company

- Several common interests, e.g. desire to sustain positive achievement record and maintain good personal relationships

- Possible complementary interests, e.g. each teams' desire to manage its own workload

With just this cursory examination of the forces, we would be justified in concluding that there is a high potential for an integrative, "win-win" solution to this issue.

Level Analysis

Differences in organizations almost always occur on many different levels. (See Figure 6.1 on page 76.) It should be apparent that differences based on some of these levels are more amenable to resolution than others. Though not true in all situations, there is typically a progression from "easier" to "more difficult" to resolve as the nature of the difference goes from the top of the list to the bottom, as the source of difference moves from superficial to deep, or rational to emotional. On the surface, this could suggest that the problem ought to be resolved at the level on which it is easiest to reach agreement. However, there is an inverse relationship between the superficiality of the solution and the degree to which it is likely to resolve the difference in an enduring way.

The utility of this information is in determining the optimum level of difference on which to focus the solution-seeking process. If it is focused very deeply, i.e. on values and beliefs or interests, needs, and motivations, it may be difficult to reach agreement, as people tend to hold onto these firmly and are less inclined to see points of view that differ from their own as valid. If it is focused at too superficial a level, the solution may fail to address the more significant causes of the problem, leading to later recurrences of the issue.

Figure 6.1: Level Analysis

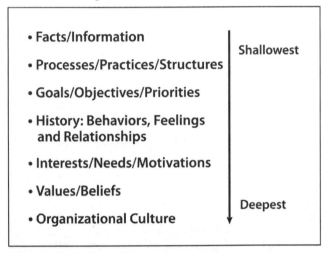

In organizational issues, it is often the case that solutions can be found by focusing on the more rational sources of the difference, as long as the deeper, more emotional ones are acknowledged and addressed in some way. To illustrate, consider the sources of difference among the software developers. Just as was apparent in the Force Field Analysis, many of the solutions lie in addressing exchange of information, structures, practices, and priorities. The relationships and personal feelings related to recent, heated exchanges will need to be acknowledged; however, in this case, these are not the most significant causes of the problem and will most likely take care of themselves when the more rational issues are resolved.

Software Development Team: Levels of Difference

Facts/Information: Each team has its own information about workload and upcoming projects; this is not shared among all teams. Neither is information shared by other parts of the organization regarding projects that can be anticipated.

Processes/Practices/Structures: The teams do not plan together. The integrator role is not clear and/or not performed well. The scarcity of resources requires sharing. The reward system rewards individuals rather than groups.

Goals/Priorities: All team members share the overarching goal of providing excellent customer service and high-quality products. Each team has its own set of priorities that may be in conflict with other team's priorities.

History re: Behaviors, Feelings, and Relationships: While generally respectful, there have been instances of raised voices and expressed anger. Close relationships outside the workplace exist among some, though not all, of the team members.

Interests/Needs/Motivations: All members want to be successful as individuals as well as wanting the department and the organization to be successful. Those who are friends outside the workplace want to preserve those relationships.

Values/Beliefs: There is a fairly strong belief on the part of some team members that it is inappropriate to express feelings of any kind in the workplace. There is also a shared value on a strong work ethic. However, at the organizational level, the value on placing blame for mistakes contributes to the problem.

Organizational Culture: There is clearly articulated emphasis on quality, precision, and accountability. Mistakes are not well tolerated, making individuals cautious and somewhat fearful.

Implications for a Strategy

Armed with information, we can now use it to form a strategy, that is, a path to get from the current situation to a more desirable solution. By reviewing all of the information and the conclusions of the three analytical processes applied, a preferred strategy has definitely emerged. First, it is apparent that it should be possible to arrive at an integrative, "win-win" solution. Second, the forces that are both significant and amenable to change are primarily structural, involving processes, practices, goals and priorities, and one related to sharing information. Other forces that may be amenable to change and potentially significant relate to behaviors and feelings. There are no issues that relate to interests, needs, and motivations or values and beliefs that are strong contenders for the focus of this resolution-seeking process. The culture of the organization, while clearly contributing to this situation, is unlikely to be amenable to change within the context of this intervention, though helping the software team to understand its impact on them is likely to be helpful.

As noted, historical events will have impacted relationships and some feelings will have been generated as a result. While it will be best if amicable relationships are ultimately restored, we believe that the process will be most successful if substantive concerns are addressed before the personal or emotional ones, for two reasons. First, the experience of working together to resolve tangible issues will have the effect of building trust and shifting relationships in a positive direction. Second, those involved will have had the opportunity to learn and practice new skills that will make it easier to address more personal or emotionally charged issues later on. Attempting to address personal issues before these things have occurred is more likely to generate discomfort or ill will, and be damaging to a constructive process.

All of these conclusions should lead to a high level of optimism about the likelihood of resolving the issue in a constructive way. However, this is still only a partial picture.

Key Learning Points

- There is benefit to be derived from thinking analytically about all of the aspects of the situation before attempting to resolve it.

- Analysis can help to determine where there is the greatest leverage for resolution and how likely it is that a win-win resolution can be attained.

- Applying analytic tools, like the three described in this chapter, helps you think rationally and strategically about the best way to approach the resolution process.

  - Force field analysis identifies the elements that exert positive and negative force to suggest which should be addressed

  - Integrative assessment considers the potential for a win-win solution

  - Level analysis assesses how deeply differences are rooted

- Save personal, relationship, and/or emotionally charged issues for a time after those involved have had the experience of working together to resolve substantive issues, as this will build trust and greater capacity for collaboration.

Skill Building Activities

For Everyone	For Managers & Leaders
Practice the three tools—Force Field Analysis, Integrative Assessment, and Level Analysis—on a real situation.	Assess the degree to which your team possesses the skills to do rational analyses using these and other tools.
Identify at least two colleagues involved in the situation. Share your analysis with them and ask them for their thoughts. What did all of you learn?	• Would training be helpful? If so, how can you provide it? • Would coaching be helpful for particular individuals or whole teams? In what ways do current norms encourage and facilitate the use of these practices or not?

Chapter 7: Prepare—Part Three: Know Yourself; Know Others

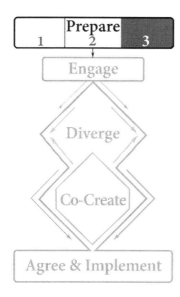

We started by noting just how complex most organizational differences are. At a minimum, there is the context provided by the organization itself, its culture, norms and practices; there is the history of the particular situation leading up to the present, including all the behaviors that have been exhibited; there are the current realities of all the parties, including yourself, consisting of motivations, interests, values, beliefs, and feelings. What opportunities are there to impact these conditions? It is unlikely that the organization will change quickly, we cannot alter what has taken place in the past, and we are generally powerless to change another person's behavior, at least in the short term. That leaves just one element over which we have considerable control: ourselves.

If that sounds straightforward, guess again. There are a large number of variables to consider in assessing our own tendencies, abilities, and choices regarding how to behave in a potentially difficult situation. And being able to make choices about your own behavior first requires a high degree of self-awareness.

Attitudes and Predisposition About Conflict

Imagine that how you approach any situation involving a difference of opinion has essentially two variables: one is the degree to which you are invested in or determined to get the outcome you want and the other is the degree to which you want to preserve a positive relationship with the other party (Thomas and Kilmann, 1974). If getting your way is of paramount importance to the extent that damage done to the relationship is immaterial, you will tend to fight very hard and be unlikely to demonstrate any flexibility. If the opposite is true and you are willing to accede in order to preserve the relationship, you will be very accommodating.

Figure 7.1 Thomas Kilmann Conflict Styles
Adapted from Thomas, K. and Kilmann, R., 1974

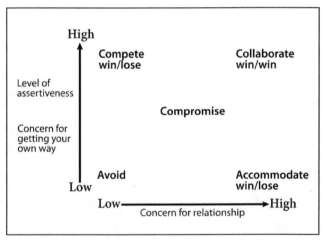

In both of these cases, there is little need to truly engage in dialogue with the other party; in the former, you use every tactic available to get them to give in to you. In the latter, you simply give in. In neither situation is it necessary to exchange much information about the reason for the position being taken, the true interests behind the positions, or the feelings or beliefs related to them. In fact, when "winning" is all that matters, it may be beneficial to withhold information about your own reasons for wanting what you want.

Suppose now that both of these variables are true to some degree—the outcome is important to you and you also wish to preserve a relatively positive relationship with the other party. If these are both true to a very great degree, you may be willing to invest a great deal of time and effort to find out all about the other person's interests, feelings, beliefs, etc. as well as sharing your own in the hope of discovering a solution that is satisfactory to all. Or both may be important, but only to the degree that you are willing to find an expedient way to negotiate an exchange in which all parties get some of what they want. Each of these strategies requires some degree of engagement.

Clearly, there are situations for which each of these approaches to resolving a difference is appropriate. When the stakes are high and there is a good potential for an integrative solution, as we defined it in the last chapter, it is generally worth the time to exchange information and work together to find that "elegant" solution that satisfies all parties' interests. This is frequently the case in organizational differences that involve individuals, teams or departments that must work together continually to provide something that is of value to the organization. When the stakes are not quite as high and time is of the essence, the expedient solution or compromise might be most appropriate. Compromise solutions are best in situations for which there is not a truly integrative "win-win" solution available or the stakes are not high enough to merit the time it takes to generate a fully collaborative, integrative solution. The difference is that in the compromise solution no one gets all of their interests fully met and the solution may be less beneficial for the organization in the long run.

There are also occasions that call for accommodating to another, as when you choose to "lose the battle to win a larger battle or to win the war," or when the outcome is far more important to one party than the other and concessions can be made without significant negative consequences. There are also those relatively rare occasions in which the outcome is so important that the relationship is secondary to the importance of one party's interests being dominant. The determination of which approach is appropriate can be aided by the information and analysis that was discussed in the last chapter.

Recognizing Your Preferred Approach

While each approach is appropriate in different instances, many people have a tendency or predisposition to rely on one approach over the others, regardless of the situation. When this is the case, the choice of what to do in a given situation is not a choice at all—it is an unconscious reaction which may or may not represent the best approach.

We have all known people who continually accommodate to others. They are unlikely to assertively express their own viewpoint or engage in a give and take about the reasons behind their wants or explore opposing viewpoints. They give way easily as soon as an opposing view is expressed. People who do this regardless of how strongly they feel about the situation often feel taken advantage of and resentful. In addition, solutions to differences in which these people are participants are likely to not solve the whole problem or be lasting.

There are also those who will "go to the mat," fighting as hard as they can to get their own way, regardless of the appropriateness of that approach to the situation. People who continually engage in behaviors like drawing a line in the sand, or firmly standing their ground until others back down, over time teach others to stay away or find a way around them. Situations in which these people are involved are also likely to go unresolved as others avoid addressing them.

A third type of non-engaging behavior involves avoiding addressing differences altogether, even when there are significant consequences. People who are perennial avoiders are often so conflict averse that they will minimize important differences and convince themselves that the problem will go away by itself. Of course that rarely happens. While there are some situations for which at least temporary avoidance may be appropriate, the person who is a persistent avoider often causes a logjam of unresolved issues.

Most people have learned to rely on one of these three "fight or flight" strategies to some extent, through early experiences in their families. Later, most of us learn the more engaged strategies of working to find true win-win, collaborative solutions or negotiating to a compromise solution. Ideally, we are all able to execute all five strategies and can make a conscious choice to use the approach that best fits the situation.

We have encountered many situations in which an individual's strong predisposition to approach differences in a particular way has led to poor outcomes. Often, in these instances, simply becoming aware of one's tendencies can lead to improvements.

The relationship between the VP of Corporate Public Relations and the CEO had become very strained. While being coached, it became clear that the VP had a strong tendency to compete, i.e. to fight hard to get her point heard and considered, and a secondary preference for accommodating. She illustrated this by saying that when she and the CEO disagreed about something she frequently got to a place of saying to herself "Why bother, she's not going to really consider my point of view," before even trying to make her case. The CEO told us that she valued the VP's advice and often used her as a sounding board for challenging situations, but that recently the VP had seemed withdrawn and resentful.

With a new insight that her learned response to differences involved the thought, "If I can't get my way I throw up my hands and give up," the VP realized that there was a better way to interact with her boss. She could formulate and present her ideas, knowing that it was the CEO's style to push back, and that this was not a rejection of her or her ideas. She could be ready to skillfully help the CEO consider and assess the options.

This kind of awareness can be even more powerful when individuals in a group learn about their tendencies.

Assessments of the tendencies of the seven software engineers and their boss who were introduced in Chapter 4 revealed the following: No one in the group had a strong predisposition to compete. This "fight" mode was the least preferred for the boss, whose first choice was to collaborate. Three of the eight had "avoid" as their first choice. When presented with this information, the team could better understand the dynamics that often took place. When a collaborative or compromise solution to differences could not be reached quickly and easily, the difference was likely to be ignored as no one was willing to advocate strongly for his own interests and was more interested in preserving harmony than finding a solution. The boss was among the least likely to choose to address difficult issues. Over time, rather than leading to harmony, unresolved issues led to feelings of frustration and resentment.

Recognizing Other Tendencies or Predispositions

By this time, you may be starting to recognize some of your own tendencies relative to "fight, flight, or engage" approaches to dealing with differences. These may be learned behaviors and they may also relate to more embedded personality preferences.

As we mentioned above, being in conflict with another person brings us face to face with a difficult choice: Do we place more value on maintaining a harmonious relationship, even if it is superficially so, than on getting the outcome we want or vice versa—are we willing to jeopardize short-term harmony in favor of trying to get our preferred outcome? For most people, the balancing act between these two choices is inherently uncomfortable because most of us want both: We want interpersonal relationships to be pleasant and we want to get our own way and be in control. When faced with a difference, we must make a choice.

Relationship Versus Outcome; Emotions Versus Logic

Some people are so uncomfortable with the idea of disrupting the harmony that they become perennial accommodators or avoiders. These people may also have a tendency to consider people's feelings over rational considerations when solving problems and making decisions.[5] They may also have a difficult time expressing their ideas and beliefs when these are different from those that others have expressed, which may leave them feeling resentful, isolated, or marginalized. This can, in turn, generate conflict.

On the other end of this continuum are people who are very concerned with decisions being based only on rational and logical considerations. These people may also have a tendency to believe that most problems have one right solution and feel that being right is very important, and outweighs any considerations regarding relationships. People with these tendencies may become easily angered or annoyed when others don't see things their way, which also tends to generate conflict.

Most of us lean toward one end or the other on this continuum. It can be helpful to know where you are so that you can check the appropriateness of your feelings and behaviors for each situation. Just increasing awareness about these tendencies makes a difference in ultimately becoming more intentional about the choices you make.

---

5   For those familiar with the Myers Briggs Type Indicator (MBTI), these tendencies correspond to the "T" and "F" on the "Thinking–Feeling" dimension which relates to choices in decision making.

Engagement Versus Closure

Similarly, on one end of another continuum, some people are very comfortable with staying engaged with others in the kind of in-depth conversation required to work through an issue collaboratively. They enjoy the give and take, and accept the time it takes to arrive at a solution that solves the problem effectively as well as preserving the relationship, and they are able to remain open to multiple possibilities. On the other end are people who are impatient with such a process, uncomfortable with the amount of time it takes to reach closure, and uncomfortable with having to maintain an openness to all perspectives.[6]

In fact, when we are engaged with another person in an effort to find a mutually satisfying relationship to a difference, we are actually in a relationship with that person, at least for the moment. This in itself can be uncomfortable for some people, particularly those who believe there is no place for feelings or relationships in organizations. As we heard from one supervisor in a technology organization, *"Emotions are not for the workplace. If you take it personally, you cannot survive. There are many things that would bother me if I heard them at home that I don't allow to bother me at work."*

Such an attitude may interfere with this individual's willingness to engage with others in search of collaborative, integrative solutions, especially when these have any degree of emotional element.

Simply knowing yourself and recognizing your own tendencies, preferences, and comfort levels can make a difference in your ability to expand your behavioral repertoire. Knowing your default behaviors can alert you to the need to pause and question yourself when entering into a situation involving differences.

---

6   This distinction relates to the "Judging–Perceiving" dimension of the Myers Briggs Type Indicator.

Attitudes About the Situation

Just as you learned everything you could about the other party's attitudes toward the situation in preparation for engaging with them, you also must become aware of your own. Of course you can only speculate about what is going on inside another person's head and heart. You can become very aware of all the things you are thinking and feeling if you commit to doing so with complete honesty.

There are several conversations you can have with yourself.

The "What's at Stake" Conversation

Situations frequently have many levels of meaning to those experiencing them. On the surface, a situation may appear to be about one thing but when you dig deeper you find that there are other things going on. Before engaging with others, it is important to understand all of the dimensions of what the issue is really about for you.

Andy believed that his disagreement with Martin, his boss, was about how they would execute a particular strategy related to publicizing a new policy to employees. Andy wanted the policy to be broadly announced with many opportunities for two-way conversations between employees and management. Martin believed the information should be relayed in a low-key way by employees' immediate managers.

On another level, the issue for Andy was really about his relationship with Martin and his feelings about his future with the company. He felt that this was yet another indication that his philosophy was not in synch with Martin's, and possibly with the entire organization. Though he didn't really want to think about it, he was beginning to question whether or not he could continue to be successful in this job, or if he ought to begin to look outside the company for other opportunities.

The "What Am I Feeling" Conversation

Most of us are out of touch or unaware of our feelings to some degree some of the time. While we may be aware of feelings when they are intense, there is a whole array of feelings that can be subtle. It is also quite possible to experience feelings without being aware of what they are related to or why we feel that way. Being aware of feelings and having a good understanding of why we have them can be extremely helpful in working through a difference.

> Andy was feeling quite anxious about this situation. He had hoped that this job would provide opportunities for advancement, not to mention job security. His position paid quite well and he was unsure that he could find anything else as good. His young family was very comfortable and settled, and they did not want to move.
>
> He was also feeling some disappointment and even sadness that yet again he was at odds with his boss. He liked Martin on a personal level but was losing respect for his professional competency, which left him feeling that the door to promotion might be locked. He felt resentful that Martin didn't trust him enough to let him have more influence and autonomy in making these decisions.

The "What Do I Really Want and Why" Conversation

> As Andy thought more about the situation, his true interests and motivation became more apparent. After almost ten years in this profession, he wanted the opportunity to prove himself. While proud of his accomplishments, he felt considerable disappointment that he had not achieved the level of responsibility he had hoped he would by this time. Most importantly, it was important to him to know that his growing expertise and years of good service to the company were being recognized and that he could expect further opportunities and rewards if he chose to stay. He began to formulate some ideas of

alternate paths that might be open to him, were he to consider other companies. He also thought about what he would lose—stable employment, colleagues he was comfortable with, and a community that his family felt a part of. He realized these concerns would have to be weighed against the "what's at stake" and "what I'm feeling" conversations to help him decide the best strategy and approach for the real conversation with Martin. He did not want to alienate or offend Martin in any way but he felt it was time for a very honest conversation.

In summary, being as clear as you can be about your own feelings, thoughts, and motivations regarding the situation will allow you to formulate a way to proceed that is not reactive and emotional but proactive and rational. This is NOT the same as having a specific position about the outcome that you want; it is to become very clear about your own interests.

Speculation About What's Most Important to Others

Now that you've gotten very clear about your own thoughts and feelings, you may be better equipped to speculate about what is true for the other person. We use the word "speculate" because you can never really know for sure what is true for someone else unless they tell you. That said, you probably can intuit some of what they may be thinking and feeling based on many things you know:

- Your knowledge of them personally—what they seem to value, believe, care about, their past behavior

- Your knowledge of the organizational context—especially what the organization rewards them for, what outcomes and metrics matter to them

- Your knowledge of the specific situation and what they have done in the past in this or similar situations

Based on an objective, non-judgmental review of these observations, you can generate some hypotheses about their motivations, interests, wants, etc. Most importantly, you will begin to gain insight into what is behind their position. This objectivity will help you approach the situation in a more neutral way, which, as you will learn in the next few chapters, is key to constructive resolution.

Figure 7.2: Example of an Analysis of a Conflict Worksheet

	Issues	Interest	"Best Outcomes"
From my own point of view			
From the other's point of view			
From the organization's point of view			

You can use this simple template to begin to analyze the situation from several points of view: your own, the others involved, and from the larger perspective of what the organization as a whole values. When you engage in this kind of analysis, you are beginning to shift your thinking away from either–or adversarial approaches to more collaborative ways of thinking. When you consider not only your own interests, but those of others, and those of the larger organization, you are moving toward a way of thinking that is consistent with the ideas presented in Chapter 2, when we discussed the application of game theory and "Tit-for-Tat" strategies into our real world, in which assumption number one is:

Apply a long-term perspective: Always assume that there is the greatest potential for your own success when there is mutual long-term success.

Using these tools also helps you to get "above the cornfield," to truly see and appreciate the big picture of what is involved in this conflict as opposed to seeing down only your own narrow perspective (or row of corn). This is the most important purpose of the *Prepare* phase of resolving differences. When you have completed all of the information gathering, analysis, and reflection, you are almost ready to *Engage*.

Human Motivation—One More Frame to Consider

Figure 7.3: A New Version
of Maslow's Hierarchy of Needs

It can be helpful to apply a theory of human motivation to better understand what might be at the root of someone's willingness to cooperate with others even when they seem to want very different things. Building on the work of Abraham Maslow, we can think of motivation existing as a hierarchy of needs, meaning that people are motivated to fulfill lower-level needs before they can focus on higher-level needs. The most basic needs are associated with survival and include physical and psychological survival. In other words, when someone's survival is truly threatened or they believe it is threatened, they are unlikely to be as concerned with higher-order needs like being accepted. Next on the hierarchy is the need to thrive, which is based on one's identity, both in terms of how one is perceived by others and one's own self-perception or self-esteem. The third level of needs relates to success and can be defined as achievement if measured against a standard or, if measured in relation to others, can be defined as winning, prevailing, or dominating. What is most salient for anyone at any given time depends on many variables.

To illustrate how levels of needs might play out in an organizational dispute, consider this example:

Susan had been hired as an intern and, much to her relief, was eventually asked to join the company in a permanent position. This job was very important to her, both as a source of income and as a stepping stone to what she hoped would be her career. The only fly in the ointment was that her new position called for her to work closely with Eileen, an older woman with whom she had frequently clashed and for whom she had little respect. Eileen had been at the company for many years and Susan perceived her to be very closed to any new ideas, particularly when they came from her.

Eileen, who had climbed the ladder to her current position over many years, was proud of her accomplishments and the respect she had earned. She was dedicated to the success of the company and was very focused on the project she was now heading, which she saw as a great opportunity to move the company toward its strategic vision. She also knew that it was an opportunity for her to be more visible to the CEO. Susan, the intern who had been assigned to the project and was now being hired full time, was bright enough but she needed a lot of coaching and seasoning, and she was taking up more time than the contribution she could make was worth.

These two are at significantly different levels in the hierarchy, which is part of what is creating an obstacle to their ability or willingness to find common ground. Susan's focus is on physical survival (income) and identity as defined by others' perception of her. Eileen is most concerned with success, both in terms of her own achievement and the possibility of winning a promotion.

Using this frame can help to further understand your own and another person's true interests. Knowing that there is a discrepancy in level of need between the two can prove an important element in determining what is needed to bring about a constructive resolution.

Prepare to Share Information

In addition to having shifted your mindset from adversarial to collaborative, from short-term and narrow to long-term and broad, and judgmental to neutral (realistically this shift is only to a degree), you have also done yourself and others a service by gathering the information that will allow others to see the big picture as well. It will be helpful to put the information together in a way that will serve that purpose.

Using only information that all involved would agree is accurate, assemble the facts and data so that it can be reviewed and easily digested and understood by others. Be very careful not to confuse opinion with fact! Do not introduce as data or fact anything that may be disputed or cannot be supported. Once you have sifted through all of the information you have collected, organize it into a form that can be presented to others for review. This will save all of you from either having to defer the conversation while more information is gathered—or worse—to proceed based on untested assumptions or speculation. Everyone will appreciate your preparation and this will enhance others' good will toward you—a great advantage!

Key Learning Points

- Your own behavior, in a situation that involves other people, is the one variable over which you have the most control.

- The more you understand about your own tendencies and preferences, the more choices you have about how to behave.

Skill Building Activities

For Everyone	For Managers & Leaders
Take the Thomas–Kilmann Conflict Mode Inventory. Share the results with someone who knows you well to validate and get feedback.	To what extent do we provide training that would enable greater self-awareness? How could we do more of this?
Identify a conflict situation you've been involved in:	To what extent do our current norms and values support the development of greater self-awareness? What can I do to support these norms?
What are you aware of regarding your approach?	
What are you aware of regarding others' approaches?	Do I model self-awareness in the choices I make about my own actions and behaviors?
Which styles would you like to become more proficient at? Create an improvement plan.	Make it a goal to become an observer of myself and my impact on others.

Chapter 8

Step 2: Engage

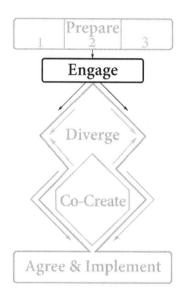

Webster's *Dictionary* defines "engage," in part, as "to offer as backing to a cause or aim; expose to risk the attainment or support of some end; to involve or entangle in some enterprise; to attract and hold; to commit or pledge; to enter into conflict." Roget's *Thesaurus* offers "take on, go up against; engross, absorb, occupy, involve." All of these definitions and synonyms imply the meaning we intend—we use the word very intentionally to mean *fully participate by being fully present in every way*.

It takes more than just showing up in the same place to create the conditions that make constructive engagement possible. It takes thoughtful planning. There are several stages needed to create the conditions for constructive engagement:

- Reframe the issue
- Invite the right people in
- Consider logistics
- Set the tone by modeling
- Share information

Reframe the Issue

To "reframe" an issue means to re-state it in a way that makes it *our* problem to solve collectively rather than a problem that pits your wants and interests against mine. It moves from a statement that poses an "either-or" problem to a statement that asks "How can we solve this problem in the best possible way, for you, for me, and for the organization?"

Example:

Either–or statement: "Should your team or my team have responsibility for this new product?"

Reframed statement: "How can we provide oversight for the new product in a way that uses both of our team's resources and expertise most efficiently and effectively?"

The first purpose of reframing is to make it attractive to the other party to engage with you in a constructive way and to avoid getting sucked into a contest of wills from the very beginning. Think about the example above. Suppose you and I are battling about which team is going to take on this new responsibility—and both of us want the other to get "stuck" with it because our plate is already too full for the perceived scarce resources we possess. We both know that there are members of our respective teams who have the expertise needed on the new project, though it would be difficult for each to release them from current assignments. I approach you with the first question above—"Which team is going to take responsibility for the new product?" Your first reaction is to start telling me all the reasons your team cannot possibly do it, how thin you are already stretched, the pressing deadlines you are facing, etc. My response to you will be to tell you why my team can't do it and how you are so much better equipped, etc. And we are off and running, locked in an either-or, attack-and-defend pattern. It is unlikely that either of us will think in terms of what is best for the organization, and we certainly won't share any information, like an accounting of what resources we actually have that might work against what we believe to be our favored solution.

Alternatively, I can approach you with a question that invites you to work with me to solve a mutual problem together rather than pitting us against one another. The seemingly simple act of stating that invitation in a way that considers the larger issue as well as acknowledging what is at stake for both of us makes all the difference. We now have an opportunity to find a solution that is good for you, good for me, and for the organization, and to actually enhance our relationship in the process. We have shifted the focus from winning and losing, right versus wrong, you versus me, to finding the best possible solution.

There are additional benefits to reframing. As happened during the preparation phase, the thought process involved in reframing allows us to adopt a more objective "above the cornfield" view of the issue. By offering up this new way of looking at it, we effectively move the other person toward this view as well. Another, more substantive, benefit is the ability later in the process to use the thinking that went into forming the reframed statement to craft a shared vision for the future that will emerge as the best agreeable solution. The reframing process also will have contributed to identification of objective criteria for assessing potential solutions.

The "Reframing Formula"

There is a formula for reframing that is based on the information you gathered about your own interests, the likely interests of the other party, and the larger interests of the organization, which is understood and shared by both of you. Although at this stage you may not know all of the other party's interests, you probably know some of them. It is also likely that some of the interests are the same and some are different.

Figure 8.1: Reframing Formula

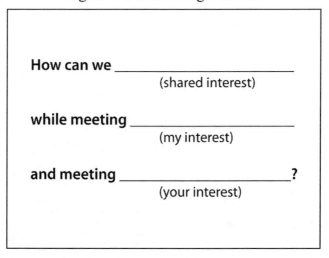

Using the example posed above, the thought process for reframing would work like this:

<u>My Interests</u>

- Use resources I have (staff time and expertise) to their best advantage
- Meet all goals and deadlines of current projects and satisfy customers
- Provide development opportunities for new junior staff members
- Avoid assigning overtime
- Contribute to the success of the new product

Other's Interests

- Use resources to their best advantage
- Exceed metrics on current most visible project X
- Add headcount to staff an important project more effectively
- Contribute to the success of the new product

Overlapping Interests

- Use current resources to best advantage
- Desire to contribute to success of new product

Different Interests

- My concern for developing new staff and avoiding overtime
- Your concern regarding performance on project X and need for more staff

Larger Organizational Shared Interests

- Desire for new product to succeed
- Shared responsibility for meeting common group or department or organizational goals

To generate a reframed statement of the issue, use the information above to fill in the "formula:"

For this situation, the reframed statement becomes:

How can we best contribute to the success of the new product, allow both of us to use our resources most effectively, avoid overtime for my staff and help me develop my new staff members and support your need to exceed metrics on project X?

While this may appear complex and may not exemplify the most correct grammatical structure, it accomplishes several things. It lets you know that I already understand your interests and believe they are legitimate. It demonstrates my willingness to disclose information about my own interests and, most importantly, it invites you to work with me as a partner to find mutually satisfying solutions to a shared problem.

> *Don, the head of a sales organization had an ongoing conflict with the head of another department whose organization was in charge of developing external partnerships with vendors who also sold their products. In Don's view, partnerships were being created with a view toward short-term goals rather than serving the long-term interests of the company. He felt his efforts to date had not been successful in trying to convince the other person to change his criteria for selecting partners.*

> *Wanting a different outcome, Don decided to change his tactics. At the next meeting, he presented a series of Microsoft PowerPoint slides that laid out his interest in becoming "aligned in common goals" to: 1) drive top-line revenues for the department; 2) establish long-term, successful relationships with channel partner; 3) ensure operational efficiency; and 4) make sound decisions that make good business sense for the company. He went on to acknowledge the interests of both groups—those that were the same and some that were not. He then posed the question: How can we together achieve success in growing our business, with long-term, successful partners? And he suggested that the goals of the meeting should be to "set clear objectives, have an honest and open dialogue, and define a clear partner plan that would satisfy everyone's interests." Don wrote back to us, saying "the meeting went better than expected as a result of reframing the proposal and focusing on our common ground. We still have work to do but were able to make significant progress in gaining buy-in, support, and consensus."*

Take a moment to practice writing a reframed problem statement for a conflict in which you are involved using the "formula."

As noted in Chapter 3, alignment around expressed organizational purpose, vision, strategy, and goals is key to finding shared interests. Common goals at department and team levels make it even more likely that shared interests among individuals will be apparent.

Invite the Right People

Who are the "right" people? Depending on the nature and complexity of the issue, there may be benefits to inviting many people to join in the search for a constructive resolution. The greater the complexity of the issue, the more likely it is that input from many will lead to a valuable solution. It is also true that there will be more support for the solution, and the actions that will need to be taken, from those who have participated in its development. On the other hand, the more people involved, the more points of view will have to be considered, making the process more challenging. Therefore, it is important to consider the reasons for inviting in the people whose presence will most likely contribute to a constructive outcome.

Consider the following criteria when deciding who to include:

Who has the information? Having all of the relevant facts about the situation will make it more likely that a valuable and sustainable solution is reached, so anyone who is in possession of essential information should be considered. Some information can be presented without the information "owner/expert" present, but information supplied by someone who is credible clearly carries more weight and makes it more likely that it will be accepted. It is also likely that those who own relevant information care about the issue. They may feel the facts were misrepresented without their being there to present them, and therefore may feel resentful if not invited. (See below—who else will be impacted?)

Who has the skill and temperament to participate in a constructive way? No, this is not "rocket science" and it might be tempting to assume that everyone can be a constructive participant in collaborative conflict resolution. Most of us know from experience that this is not the case. There are three basic desirable characteristics to look for:

Ability to see and care about the big picture: True, the majority tend to think first in terms of our own narrow and immediate self-interest. Yet most are capable of seeing the larger context and understanding the trade-offs that sometimes must be made to create a better outcome for everyone in the long run. Some people have a harder time doing this than others. If you know that some potential participants have an extremely difficult time letting go of their own need to be "right" or to "win" to retain their power, that may be a good reason to exclude them (as long as they are not likely to become an obstacle later on.)

Ability to listen to others: Again some people have a more difficult time than others to stop talking long enough to really hear what others have to say. People who are non-stop talkers who seldom listen with an interest in understanding another viewpoint can disrupt a constructive process.

Ability to express one's own point of view and actively participate: We all know people who are so uncomfortable stating their own views that they tend to remain silent even when they have something to add. The most valuable participants are those who are willing to take the risk of saying what they think or believe even if it may be unpopular.

Who has the ability to decide? It is best if the person or people who will ultimately decide what solution to adopt are present and involved. If those individuals are not active participants, they will not be able to appreciate the full flavor of the deliberations, all that was considered and how various individuals felt about the issues—and therefore will not be able to base the decision on those subtleties. There are, of course, instances in which this is not possible, as when a decision will be made by a board or executive who is unavailable. When that is the case, involving people who are as close as possible to the decision maker is advised.

Who else will be impacted, whose support is needed for implementation and who could block implementation? Anyone who will be impacted by the solution can be thought of as having a vested interest in the proceeding and its outcome. While you don't want to include so many people that the process becomes impossible to manage, you do not want to leave anyone out who will resent having been left out to the extent that they will not support the decision or will actively block its implementation. While it might be tempting to exclude the people who you know have strong opinions or are opposed to the outcome you may favor, this is rarely a good criterion, even though it may violate some of the other criteria outlined above.

Consider and Plan Logistics

Timing may be everything but it is only one of the things to consider in planning the logistics of an engaged meeting. The principle to follow is that a sense of neutrality is conveyed and all of the factors that might be important to the people you've invited to participate are considered. Logistical factors include:

Schedule: Others should be consulted regarding scheduling of meetings, and attempts should be made to maximize convenience for all participants. Meeting duration should be clearly defined and adhered to. It can be challenging to get everyone to agree to spend the considerable amount of time that thoughtful deliberation requires. We advise scheduling no less than a two-hour block of time for the first meeting. It may be easier to get others to agree to the necessary amounts of time for subsequent meetings once they have experienced the first one.

Location: Ideally, the location should not only be convenient for everyone but also quiet, private, comfortable, and neutral. By neutral, we mean it is not more comfortable and convenient to some parties than to others.

Space and Seating: The space should be comfortable and well-lit. Round tables are ideal for this kind of interaction; they allow everyone to see everyone else and no one is made to feel dominant or subordinate by virtue of the seating arrangement.

Tools: We favor the use of easels with chart pads and markers. These allow everyone to view the thoughts, ideas, and suggestions that are made, which makes misunderstanding less likely. Taking the time to write things out also serves to slow things down, encouraging time for reflection. When there is a lot of information to be conveyed, the use of PowerPoint and printed handouts can be helpful. Everyone should be asked to bring materials for making their own notes.

Set the Tone by Modeling Behaviors

Perhaps the most effective tools you have to help you in reaching constructive, collaborative outcomes to conflicts are your own behaviors. We sometimes experience people's cynicism about the likelihood that the "others" will participate willingly and in good faith in constructive conflict resolution. We understand that there is good reason for cynicism! Most of us can tell many stories about conflict that has escalated, turned ugly, or simply dragged on forever because of someone's stubbornness, competitiveness, hunger for power … an endless litany of human flaws.

Our response to this understandable feeling is that we cannot change another person's behavior directly. What we can do is change our own behavior in ways that make it almost impossible for the other person not to change his or hers. These behaviors include the following:

Reflect an attitude of optimism and openness: Approach the situation in a way that says "I believe that we can resolve this issue in a constructive way." This might involve acknowledging how difficult and challenging it is, understanding that there is much at stake, that you are far apart in your preferences, etc., and continuing to express optimism about the likelihood of a constructive outcome for all, nonetheless. Along with this optimistic mindset, convey that you are open to considering many alternatives and that you have a desire to truly under-stand the other person's point of view. When others experience your optimism and openness, they are very likely to begin to suspend their own cynicism about the situation. They may not entirely agree or even believe you, but they will be sufficiently disarmed that their mindset will already have shifted just a bit.

Convey trust in the other's motives: "I know you want to resolve this just as much as I do and that you care about the outcome being beneficial for the organization as well as for yourself, just as I do" is a good opening statement. By giving them the benefit of the doubt about their own motivations, you effective-ly lure them into behaving in a cooperative way. Even if they think you are nuts or naïve to trust them, they are much more likely to proceed in a non-aggressive way from the beginning.

Suspend judgments: When we make judgments about what another person is saying, we often misunderstand the informa-tion or don't really hear it at all. Setting aside judgments allows you to take in new information that you might otherwise miss. Approach the situation with an open mind and convey this in your behavior. Use descriptive rather than evaluative language. For example, say "I think it is important for us to try to listen to each other so we can really understand one another's views" instead of "You never listen to me." Practice keeping your mind open and neutral, as you listen to the other person's views, even if you disagree. This does not mean that you give up your own views, only that you understand the other person's as well.

Check assumptions: We all make many assumptions as we go through our day. In fact, it would be impossible to make no assumptions; assumptions are what allow us to use past knowl-edge and information to predict what will happen in a given situation. Making assumptions causes problems when two people make different assumptions about the same situation. This happens because we all experience the world differently. Particularly in conflict situations, unchecked assumptions can lead to poor outcomes. It is important to establish a norm that assumptions will be checked out whenever possible. Checking out an assumption is as easy as saying "Tell me what you mean by that" or "What is the source for that information? How could we validate that?"

Acknowledge emotions while not behaving emotionally: Emotions are real; what we feel and what the other person feels are part of the reality of the situation. If there has been some negative emotion generated by the situation, it is best to acknowledge it. For example, "I know we've both been very frustrated by this situation" or "I must admit I've felt pretty angry about this and it wouldn't surprise me if you have too." Both of these sentences acknowledge feelings; and they do so in a very calm and non-emotional way. Doing so allows us both to move on and deal with each other calmly and rationally. Not acknowledging them may raise the emotion in a way that could get in the way of a constructive exchange because felt emotions that are not acknowledged can creep into our tone of voice or other non-verbal behaviors. Allowing negative emotions to be expressed in words or tone or gestures is an almost certain way to sabotage a constructive exchange. Talking about feelings this way may not come naturally; practicing creating this kind of language can help.

Establish norms explicitly by creating "ground rules": Whether you call them ground rules or "agreements about how we'll work on this together," it is very effective to explicitly introduce a set of practices or behaviors. Stating them out loud and putting them in writing makes it much more likely that the process will be constructive. Once stated, they can be referred to, tactfully and as a gentle reminder, whenever someone does something that violates one of them.

Share Information

Have you ever been in a meeting in which everyone's valuable time is spent arguing about the accuracy or validity of information that could easily have been verified, had someone take the time to do so before the meeting? We find this often to be the case. Sometimes, no one did it because they assumed everyone "knew" the same things they "knew," never considering that others might have different perspectives or recollections. Sometimes, people confuse their own opinion with "fact," and do not consider that there are relatively simple ways to validate what is fact and what is not.

Figure 8.2 An Example of Ground Rules

- *Be Interested:* Listen to and respect all points of view
- *Be Accepting:* Suspend judgments as much as possible
- *Be Curious:* Seek to understand rather than persuade
- *Be Open-Minded:* Question assumptions and look for new insights
- *Remain Rational:* Focus on issues rather than the personal
- *Be Sincere:* Speak authentically and honestly about what has meaning
- *Be Brief:* Spend more time listening than talking
- *Be Civil:* Speak as you would wish to be spoken to

Of course, not everything can be validated; some things are truly subjective or based on a particular value, belief, interest, etc. There is value in sharing information that all can agree is factual. Taking the time to locate valid information and making it available before or during the meeting saves not only time but eliminates some unnecessary sources of conflict.

One of our coaching clients was helped to resolve a long-standing conflict by a process that included many of the elements of "engagement:"

The editor of a major magazine had worked for several months to justify a reorganization of her department to the president. Other key executives had also been involved in multiple meetings, including the CFO and his assistant, the editor-in-chief, and the VP of Human Resources. Despite the editor being engaged in outside coaching assistance to help format the justification, the editor continued to be unsuccessful in gaining agreement to move forward with the proposed reorganization and resulting position and headcount changes.

After several months of no progress and growing frustration, the coaches suggested that they facilitate a meeting with the president and key executives and assist the editor in her presentation. A one-hour meeting was granted. The president arrived approximately 15 minutes late and announced that she only had the originally planned time available. The coaches facilitated the discussion in a very planned and controlled way, beginning with a list of proposed "ground rules" such as, avoid interruptions, listening for understanding, no questions until the editor's presentation was fully completed, etc.

After agreeing to the process and ground rules, the editor made her presentation. Following the uninterrupted presentation, questions were raised. Having fully listened (probably for the first time) to the editor's presentation and looking at her clearly documented headcount numbers, etc., one executive observed that these numbers were different than had been assumed all along.

The president asked a few questions for clarification and quickly agreed to the reorganization proposal and the resulting headcount changes.

The meeting concluded, with an affirmative decision, in less than the scheduled time.

Key Learning Points

Setting the stage for a constructive engagement requires thoughtful attention to many factors:

- State the issue in a way that makes everyone care about how it will be resolved and makes them believe that their interests and concerns will be considered.

- Decide who to involve based on knowing who has relevant information, who can help or hinder implementation of the solution, and whose participation will be most constructive. Avoid either too few or too many participants.

- Plan logistics—time, place, seating arrangement etc.—in a way that is most comfortable for the most people involved.

- Model behaviors and attitudes that will contribute to a constructive process, i.e. optimism, openness, trust, neutrality, clarity, calmness even while acknowledging emotions.

- Establish ground rules that spell out these kinds of helpful behaviors and ask others to adhere to them.

- Provide as much relevant information as possible that can be agreed to as valid by all involved. Present it as early in the process as you can to establish a common starting point and avoid arguing over facts that can be validated.

Skill Building Activities

For Everyone	For Managers & Leaders
Choose an example situation you have been or currently are involved in. Practice:	For situations in which your subordinates are involved in conflict, determine what is the most appropriate role for you to play:
• Outlining your own interests;	
• Describing what you believe to be others' interests;	• Step in and resolve the problem for them;
• How are these different from positions?	• Encourage them to resolve it themselves, stay hands-off;
Write a reframed problem question/statement.	• Encourage them to resolve it and offer to help if needed.
Define what elements will make for the most constructive process:	• Request third-party help from HR or other internal or external resources.
• Who should be involved? In what way?	Help others become more skillful in resolving differences by offering training and/or coaching.
• Where and when should you meet?	
• What ground rules should be established?	Develop additional resources to help others improve their skills.
How will relevant information be shared?	Create spaces that are conducive to constructive interaction and problem solving.
	Allow time for constructive processes to take place.

Chapter 9

Step 3: Diverge

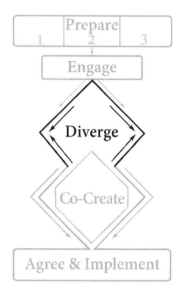

Defining and Embracing Differences

The groundwork has been done, the stage is set, and the protagonists are beginning to do the work of finding resolution to their differences. It's time to put some of the lessons learned thus far into action.

The intent of this step is to bring the differences among parties into sharp focus. It is not intended to even begin to try to resolve or reconcile the differences, but rather to simply identify, acknowledge, and embrace them. It will also reveal the ways in which the parties actually are in or close to agreement. Toward these ends, this step is all about how the parties will communicate with one another in ways that encourage openness, honesty, and transparency.

It would be naïve to think that everyone comes into this step with the same level of trust or willingness to share their thoughts, wants, beliefs, and feelings, though having effectively completed Steps 1 and 2 will have already shifted some in this direction. It is through the process of give and take and *modeling* the behaviors that contribute to collaboration that this step can fulfill its promise of moving the process closer to a win-win outcome.

We use the word "Diverge" to describe this step because it does have the effect of underscoring the differences between the parties as views are expressed and clarified. It may go against the grain of some inherent tendencies to "cut to the chase" and arrive quickly at the first solution everyone can agree to, but it is an essential step for arriving at the kind of effective solutions that organizations need to be successful.

Focus on Interests Rather than Positions to Achieve Mutual Understanding

The ultimate goal of the entire process is to find the "best" solution, i.e. one that serves the larger needs of the organization for the long term, satisfies most if not all of the needs of all of the parties, and preserves or improves the relationships among those involved. Even though this is *your* goal, it is quite likely that the others involved have something else in mind. People often approach a difference having thought only about their own experience, their own understanding of the facts, and their own wants and interests. As a result, they often have come to a conclusion about what they want the outcome to be and approach the exchange as one in which they will try to convince you of the merit of their position. In this step, your intent will be to help other parties discover that there are other ways of looking at the situation so that they become willing to step back from their preconceived position. The key is to focus on the interests—what is truly important to them and to you—that underlie their preconceived idea of the "right" solution.

People also come with their own tendencies for approaching conflict in certain ways: Some are naturally competitive, others tend to accommodate; some are avoiders, and others are inclined to compromise or collaborate. You will want to encourage collaborative attitudes and behaviors, and discourage competitive, accommodating or avoidant behaviors throughout the rest of the process. Though it may be tempting to take advantage of another's tendency to simply give in to you or withdraw from the process, leaving you to act on your own behalf, this is not likely to produce an outcome that will be fully supported by others whose support you will need. You are seeking an outcome that is the product of all parties working together to find the solution that is best for everyone.

At this point, you might be thinking, "Why am I the one to be directing this toward a mutually beneficial solution when the others are most likely going to try to win me over and get the outcome they want? Isn't that a little unfair? Aren't I likely to wind up giving in and getting less than them and less than I want?" You may be tempted to abandon the approach of learning about their interests and looking for solutions that serve the greater good and go for the short-term "win." But short-term wins, while they may feel good in the moment, are rarely rewarded in the long term and almost never put an end to the conflict. Consider the following familiar scenario:

Sam and Ralph both headed up project teams within an operations department, and frequently had to compete for projects and for the resource needed to complete them successfully. They also often shared the same resources. Sam's approach tended to be much more competitive than Ralph's, so Sam sometimes got what he wanted even when it wasn't in the best interests of the organization. Over time, Ralph became resentful of Sam and began to make negative comments about him; eventually, both teams began to see each other as "the enemy." As employees fell in behind their bosses, the lack of cooperation across teams led to hoarding of resources, which impacted each team's ability to perform.

Morale and productivity suffered in both groups and in the organization.

A different outcome is possible. The two protagonists could create a process in which they become partners in the search for the solution that is most beneficial for all involved *in the long run*. This does not require either to sacrifice his interests. That would also not be of service to the organization, because the best, most implementable and enduring solutions are likely to come from an honest and thorough examination of all the information, all of the perspectives, views, and interests of those involved. Rather, it provides the opportunity for all parties to express their views and interests and have the satisfaction of being heard and understood. In addition, this step again enables everyone involved to gain a larger perspective of the issues and begin to move away from adherence to their own predetermined position, toward a more collaborative process and outcome. It also paves the way for all parties to accept and support the solutions that are reached, because they will have been involved in crafting them.

Attention to Both Process and Content Required

"Content" refers to what we talk about: the information, opinions, interests, ideas, etc. "Process" is the way we go about our discussion and the impact that it has on those involved. The goals of Diverge include both process and content.

Content Goals

- Increase all parties' understanding of one another's perceptions, feelings, interests, motivations, and beliefs;

- Ensure that everyone has the same set of facts and information;

- Create a shared, common understanding of the entire situation from a "big picture" perspective.

- Agree on a preliminary sorting of specific topics that will need to be resolved to bring the matter to a close.

Process Goals

- Continue to shift away from an adversarial/win-lose process toward a collaborative search for best solutions;

- Allow all parties to feel that they have been heard and understood;

- Move all parties away from focusing on their predetermined solutions (positions) to thinking about what is the best solution for the entire situation (satisfying everyone's interests).

Both kinds of goals will be addressed simultaneously. This is most likely not going to be a scripted, orderly, or linear process. Rather, it will be a conversation in which information is shared in a way that accomplishes the process goals.

The most powerful tool you have for moving the process away from adversarial and toward a collaborative, win-win problem-solving process is your own mindset, approach, and behavior. Although you may not be able to completely predict or control what happens, there is much that you can do to shape it.

As you take turns speaking and listening, there are many opportunities to influence the overall process as well as the mindset, approach, and behavior of others by your own behavior.

As Listener

Let Them Go First and Make Them Feel Heard

Always let the others take the first turn in sharing their views. This provides the opportunity for you to model good listening behavior and allows them to get their views heard. This is useful in furthering both process and content goals.

It is to your advantage, in several ways, to learn as much as you can about the other parties' interests, wants, and needs. The more you know about what they care about most, the more opportunities you will have to influence them in the next steps. *Remember,* *it is <u>not</u> the goal to try to convince them of anything in this step. Rather it is just to listen and learn and share information.*

It is also to your advantage to make them feel that they have been heard and understood. It is actually quite a rare experience to feel that someone is giving you their undivided attention. Not only will this make them feel more positive about the process and about you, it will also make it more likely that they will be willing to accord you the same opportunity to be heard when it is your turn to speak. Once someone feels that others understand their views, even if they don't agree, they have less need to continue to explain themselves and may begin to have more mental capacity to hear other views.

Listen to Understand

Adopt a mindset of "listening to understand," with genuine curiosity about what is true for them. This may sound simple but it is much more difficult than you imagine, especially when there are strong feelings and intensely held opinions involved. Listening to understand is different than the way most of us listen most of the time. Typically, when other people are speaking, we are busy judging what they are saying (Do I agree or disagree? Are they right or wrong? Where did they get that idea? etc.) and planning what we will say in response.

The difficulty we experience in listening with curiosity may be more profound for some than others, but we believe it can be learned by anyone. Some cultures have a deep respect for listening and their conversations are characterized by long pauses in between speakers because to interrupt is considered rude and unacceptable. In other cultures, speaking over one another is natural. Setting clear expectations about listening behavior, including not interrupting the person speaking, can be helpful in bridging these differences.

When we run an exercise in which people are asked to listen in this way while another person expresses an opposing view on a controversial topic, it becomes clear just how challenging it is to listen without trying to influence. While it is impossible to suppress one's own internal judge, it is possible, though not without a great deal of intent and discipline, to not externalize the judge. Keeping the non-verbal cues neutral is one of the challenges. Facial expressions, body posture and movements, and tone of voice convey judgment, often without our awareness. It takes practice and feedback to bring these into awareness and control them.

Another way we can communicate judgment or subtly try to influence the person speaking without being fully aware is in how we ask questions. Asking open-ended questions to get more information and clarifying questions to make sure we understand are all good. When truly neutral, they signal and reinforce our desire to truly understand another point of view, helping to make the other person feel heard. There can be a subtle difference between truly neutral questions (Can you tell me more about that?) and ones that are leading (Don't you think...?) Tune into yourself as you ask clarifying questions to see if they are leading or neutral.

With the mindset of "listening to understand," it will come quite naturally to ask open-ended and clarifying questions, and even to paraphrase your understanding of what they are saying back to them to check the accuracy of your understanding. All of these techniques are effective ways to learn about their views and make them feel more positive about you and about the process. You are also modeling this behavior for them, which makes it more likely that they will at least be willing to attempt to do the same when it is your turn to share your own views.

Listen With an Open Mind

Another quality of listening is "listening with a willingness to be influenced" or simply listening with an open mind. Again, this sounds easier than it is. This does not mean that you abandon your own views or beliefs. It requires the ability to hold possibly opposing views or beliefs simultaneously, by temporarily "bracketing" (putting aside) what we think we know or believe, to allow for the possibility that something else could be true. In this way we can acknowledge and accept that different individuals, due to their different experiences, may have varying versions of what is true. It also enables you to learn about the others' thinking and experience in a deeper way.

> *When the magazine editor in Chapter 5 was allowed to present her information regarding the work that her team did, the numbers of hours and overtime currently worked, and the benefits that two additional positions would create for the organization, the CEO and CFO were able to bracket their own beliefs and consider the possibility that the editor's information was correct and her conclusions warranted. Instead of arguing that she was wrong and they were right (as they had done previously), they agreed to look into the validity of the editor's version. When they did, they discovered that there was additional and relevant information of which they had been unaware. As a result, their decision was revised in a way that was beneficial to the editor, the magazine, and the company as a whole.*

While some people may find it difficult to accept that there can be more than one "truth," many recognize that every individual perceives things differently than every other individual due to the fact that we are each unique. "Perception" depends on many variables; so, when trying to resolve a difference, it is useful to understand how each person views the situation and to accept that each person believes his or her view is the accurate one. Consider eye witness reports in which several people, all viewing the same event, recall what happened quite differently. Their perception could be influenced by the angle from which they were viewing the scene, their particular cognitive ability to capture what they see and translate it into words, or the acuity of their color vision. Past experience, cultural background, and religious beliefs can all influence perception.

A common mistake most of us make is to quickly travel up a

"ladder of inference[7]" when we're listening to someone else's views. This happens when we overlay assumptions that are based on past experience to interpret observations, draw conclusions and adopt beliefs. In the example just cited, the CEO continued to make the assumption that the editor's numbers were wrong and the business manager's were correct, because she had experienced the editor as being "flighty" in the past. That assumption led her to discount new information and conclude that the editor's desire for more staff had led her to inflate the numbers. In order to fully consider the new information, she needed to question her own assumption. This is difficult to do because we rely on assumptions to help us make sense of the world. But putting them aside long enough to truly consider another point of view is necessary to expand our own views and understandings and, ultimately, to resolving differences.

Figure 9.1: Ladder of Inference

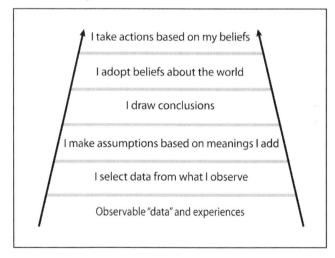

I take actions based on my beliefs

I adopt beliefs about the world

I draw conclusions

I make assumptions based on meanings I add

I select data from what I observe

Observable "data" and experiences

---

7   Ladder of Inference is a concept adopted from multiple sources. An early source is Overcoming Organizational Defenses by Chris Argyris, 1990. Allyn and Bacon, Mass.

Listening to understand and with an open mind is another way of gathering information that could be helpful in finding a solution that is agreeable to all as well as resolving the difference.

It does not mean you are agreeing that their view is correct or better than yours, only that it is different and that they believe it to be true or right. It is another way that you elevate yourself to that proverbial cornfield or balcony to get a more complete picture of the whole situation, of which their views are a part. A byproduct may well be that others are also beginning to see the same larger picture.

Don't Confuse Impact with Intent

It is natural to constantly be on alert for anything that might be potentially harmful. When harm is experienced, it is not unusual for someone to jump to the conclusion that it was caused intentionally. Though understandable, the conclusion is often incorrect and can lead to an inappropriate response that does damage to the relationship.

When someone's actions have had a negative impact on you, slow down to examine the possible reasons behind the behavior before formulating a response. Ask yourself, what might be the reasons for the actions? Could they be related to the other person's lack of information, their own fears or concerns, and not have anything to do with you? Frequently, people's actions are at worst thoughtless or insensitive and not intended to do harm.

As Speaker

When it is your turn to share your views and opinions, your goal is to inform rather than convince. Again, this difference can be subtly conveyed by the words you choose and by your non-verbal communication.

Present Your Views as if They are One Way of Seeing Things, Not the Only Way, or the "Right" Way

Make it easy for others to hear and accept your view by offering it as your perception, experience, or belief, and acknowledging that it may be different from theirs for a variety of reasons. Ask only that they accept that this is your view.

Avoid any language that could be heard as judgmental of them or their views. Use descriptive, neutral language as much as possible. Avoid saying anything that could be heard as blaming them for the problem. Use the pronoun "I" when describing your own experiences and thoughts, and talk about what you believe and why you believe it.

> When the magazine editor presented her information, she said, "Here are the numbers that I have gathered. I've noticed that they differ from [Peter's] numbers. I don't know exactly why they are different or where Peter got his numbers; I only know I personally gathered the information in the last few months and checked it with each person on my team and then checked it again with the HR Department to validate it."

She could have said something like:

> "My numbers are different from yours. I've been trying to tell you this for months but no one would listen to me. Your numbers are wrong; I don't know where they came from, but you didn't even talk to anyone on my team, and you haven't talked to HR, so how could you think they are right?"

The difference in the two presentations is visceral; the anger and frustration comes across as accusatory in the second example, while the first is neutral, calm, and non-blaming. You can imagine that they would be heard and the impact felt quite differently. The second presentation would be likely to provoke an equally frustrated and probably defensive response, making it less likely that the information itself would be heard, understood, or accepted.

Avoid Misunderstandings and Seek Clarity

Something as simple and innocent as a misunderstood word can derail a conversation. It is not unusual for individuals to differ in how they use, define, and interpret words within a given context.

> *During a team meeting, the supervisor told his team, "I don't believe I can trust you when I am not here." Several team members understood him to mean that he thought they would steal or do something clearly and intentionally wrong if he was not watching them. They were very offended and reacted very negatively. When the clamor died down, someone thought to ask what he meant. He explained that he meant he was not sure he could trust them to do the job as well or as quickly as they would when he was there, not that he thought they would intentionally do anything wrong or dangerous or illegal. Clearing up the definition of the word "trust" allowed the process to continue in a constructive way.*

In order to avoid such misunderstandings, it is important to slow the conversation down to allow for clarification. Referring back to the ground rules can be useful when encouraging everyone to be careful about making assumptions and to always ask clarifying questions when there is any doubt about the meaning of what is being said.

Vaguely defined terms can get in the way of reaching agreements. Taking time to define terms precisely during this step can be very helpful later when generating possible solutions.

> *At the strategic planning retreat, the owners of the company were repeatedly described as "risk-averse." Some of the board members thought this meant that they would vote against any acquisition that required an investment or could not be guaranteed to have a short-term, positive return on investment. Others thought it meant only that they were not willing to take a risk that could harm the company in the long term. Still others thought it only referred to the owners' unwillingness to*

take a diminished dividend at any time. Until the owners'
true desire was made clear, there could be no agreement
on strategy regarding acquisitions.

Share All Information That is Relevant

Transparency regarding what you know about the situation can help everyone to see the same big picture. It also makes it much more likely that others will share all of what they know, further enhancing the opportunities for finding effective solutions. Sharing information helps to build trust. Be careful to share information clearly either as fact—things you know are valid and not debatable—or as opinion.

Sharing what is important to you, i.e. your true interests, can also lead to ultimately more satisfying and effective outcomes. However, you must be careful to state your interests not as demands or inflexible positions, but simply as what you want and care about.

Some people believe that withholding information and not revealing what they want or care about is an effective negotiating strategy. That is not the case in constructive, collaborative approaches to resolving differences. In fact, the more everyone knows and understands about all of the interests, views, and information involved, the more likely it is that effective solutions will be reached.

Of course there is some amount of strategy necessary in the timing of all of this information sharing. We will say more about this below in the section on "Tit-for-Tat."

Manage Your Emotions

Feeling emotions, like making judgments, is unavoidable. At any given moment, we may feel a range of emotions, from anger to appreciation, from grief to joy, from triumph to humiliation. None of these is "wrong." Feelings are a natural part of the human experience. What gets us into trouble is not having feelings, but how and when those feelings get communicated.

There is a crucial difference between experiencing an emotion and expressing it outwardly. Differentiating between the two is a function of awareness, good judgment, and control. The concept of *"emotional intelligence"*[8] gives us a useful way to think about the skills and processes involved. It is a set of skills that allows us to separate the experience of feeling an emotion from taking any action as pure reaction to that experience and, rather, to make an intelligent and intentional choice about what to do. It is important here because unintentional expressions of emotion have the potential to dramatically impact the nature of any exchange.

> *The dynamic suddenly changed in the midst of what seemed to be a productive conversation between the president of a small, privately owned company and the owner of the company. When the president mentioned that a particular employee had questioned whether the owner truly supported the president in her decisions because of his observations of the owner's behavior, the owner became visibly and audibly angry. The president responded to his show of anger by refusing to continue the conversation.*

In this example, neither of these people demonstrated much emotional intelligence. Had they done so, it could have happened like this:

> *President: One of the employees told me recently that, when you are in the office, you sometimes say things in casual conversation that makes people question whether you are really supportive of the decisions I make. That makes me feel less respected by employees and that I may not have their commitment to my decisions. I would like to explore this with you and see if there is something we could agree on so that doesn't happen.*
>
> *Owner: (Feeling very annoyed at this, pauses before he*

---

8   Popularized by Daniel Goleman (*Emotional Intelligence*, 1996), this important concept has been written about extensively and is frequently included in programs for leaders and managers.

responds) I understand how this would make you feel.
It is certainly not my intent to have this impact. It also
makes me upset and a little angry that an employee
would question my motives. Let's see if we can figure out
how to avoid this in the future.

In this version, both people did several things that were helpful:

- They talked about the situation by sharing their own experience and the impact it had on them, not in a way that blamed or accused the other;

- They did express what they felt, but did so without conveying emotionality in the non-verbal behaviors they displayed;

- They made an attempt to understand and acknowledge what the other person might be feeling;

- They considered the long term impact and solution rather than getting stuck in dealing only with the immediate situation and their reactions to one another.

These are the hallmarks of emotional intelligence. Managing one's emotions effectively does not mean ignoring or suppressing them. Rather, it means being thoughtful and intentional about how, when, and whether to express them, taking into consideration everything you know about the situation and the other person, and with a desired outcome in mind. It takes practice to develop these skills, but with practice anyone can become more emotionally intelligent.

Some people are uncomfortable with emotions in any form and feel that there is no place for them in the workplace, despite considerable evidence that acknowledging feelings is a way to defuse negative expressions of them. Others may feel that they have not really been heard or validated until those around them fully understand the depths of their emotional experience. The more we know about how emotions are related to behavior, the more we understand that intentionally slowing reaction time, putting a name to the emotion, and verbalizing it all work to diminish the intensity with which it is felt. This allows a person to employ emotional intelligence in responding to a situation. Modeling this behavior for others can alter their behavior as well as your own.

Tit-for-Tat and Reinforcement Theory

All of the behaviors we've described in this chapter are conducive to creating a constructive exchange. Though others involved in the discussion may not initially behave in these ways, by acting this way yourself you are giving them a model for alternative ways of behaving. When you do this consistently, it has the effect of gently steering them to behave in a similar way.

Another way to encourage others to behave in certain ways is to apply reinforcement theory. Simply stated, this means that you respond in positive ways (verbally and non-verbally) when someone does something you want them to do, and in mildly negative ways when they do something you do not want them to do. By "rewarding" behaviors that are consistent with constructive, collaborative processes and outcomes, and "punishing" behaviors that are inconsistent with these, the other person's behavior will gradually be altered in the direction of behaving more cooperatively.

In Chapter 2, we discussed how economists and other social scientists used game theory to learn about how people behave when they have to choose between acting solely for their own immediate advantage or for a greater good, even if they might have to make a short-term sacrifice. When the game was run only once, as if the players were dealing with someone they would never have to see again, they almost always acted only on their own behalf. But when it was run multiple times, a pattern began to take shape that proved most beneficial to all players, which they called Tit-for-Tat. That pattern followed these rules: begin with a cooperative move; respond to the other player in the same way that he/she did, whether cooperative or uncooperative; return to a cooperative move. When a player adopted this strategy, the other player gradually began to act the same way, which ultimately resulted in a win-win outcome. The more rounds of the game played, the greater the chances that this pattern emerged.

This works because of reinforcement theory. The second player is rewarded for being cooperative and punished or retaliated against for not being cooperative. You can recreate this pattern by responding positively to cooperative behavior and negatively to non-cooperative behavior. A positive response could be something as simple as a non-verbal gesture like smiling or nodding or leaning forward, or it could be more substantive, like saying "Yes, I can understand your point," or "I didn't know that until now; that's interesting to know." Similarly, a negative response could be a frown or saying something like "I can't agree with you on that," or "I think you may be viewing this very narrowly." When meting out a punishing or retaliatory move, be careful that it is proportional to the offense being responded to. For example, in response to someone becoming argumentative and demanding that their position be accepted, it might be appropriate to say, "As long as you insist on your view being the only correct view, I cannot continue to accept that it has any credibility at all unless you can produce the numbers to support it." It would not be appropriate to push back by threatening to take other actions that would be damaging to them. Taking such action would most likely begin a downward spiral of retaliatory behaviors that would derail the talks.

The behavior to be reinforced is anything consistent with a collaborative process, including transparency in information sharing, good listening skills, being open to alternate views, etc. Behavior to not be reinforced ("extinguished" in behavioral terms) is anything that does not contribute to a productive process, like clinging rigidly to the correctness of one's own view, or expressing blame.

Here is an example of how this might work:

Person 1: Opens with a competitive, non-cooperative statement. This could be an aggressive statement about the merit of their position or point of view or about what is wrong with your point of view or something else equally judgmental or argumentative.

> *"I want you to stop coming into the office and talking with employees in a way that undermines my authority."*

Person 2: Responds with a statement that lets the person know that this is not an acceptable way to begin the discussion. They also offer a way to proceed that is more collaborative:

> *"I'd be glad to talk with you about this. I would appreciate it if we could both work harder at communicating without accusing one another. When you approach me with what feels like an accusation and a demand, it just makes me angry. I'm sure the same is true for you. I think there must be a better way."*

Conversely, if Person 1 opens cooperatively, by acknowledging that there is a problem and indicating a willingness to engage in a constructive process, Person 2 will respond in an equally cooperative way.

This pattern, continued throughout the remaining steps of the engagement, has the impact of shaping the other person's behavior by "rewarding" cooperative behavior and "punishing" uncooperative behavior, making a win-win outcome more likely. It is also a protection for you. It means that if you are met with a person who behaves competitively and non-cooperatively, you do not simply or naively share all of your wants, interests, feelings, and beliefs, as they could take advantage of knowing these if they have no intention of engaging in a constructive process. While this doesn't happen often if you have followed and applied all of what has been suggested so far, there are, in our experience, some individuals who are unwilling or unable to let go of their competitive, win-lose nature.

"Diverge" May Take Multiple Meetings

You will know when you have successfully completed "Diverge" when all of the parties know and understand all of the information that is relevant to resolving the issues. In some very complex problems there may need to be time between meetings for gathering more information or validating data. It is important that someone keeps track of all the information that is agreed to, what information is missing or inaccurate or questionable, and where there are real and substantive disagreements. At this point, it will be helpful to take stock of all of the themes that have emerged and do an initial sort of topics or issues to be addressed. These might be arranged by criteria such as "easy to difficult" or whatever helps to keep them organized. Be careful not to fragment the situation irrevocably, as some of the most creative and effective solutions might be holistic, spanning several categories. Assignments should be made for whatever actions are needed before the next meeting takes place, to ensure that all of the pieces of the puzzle are on the table.

Key Learning Points

- The goal of this step is to further the understanding that all parties have of one another's views, concerns, motivations, and wants. Solution-seeking or advocating for particular outcomes should not be a part of the discussion at this time.

- The tone and the focus of the exchange should be neutral, open—even curious—and non-evaluative. By modeling these behaviors, others may follow suit.

- Being listened to without interruption, without evaluation or interpretation, only to be understood, is a powerfully positive experience. By listening to others in this way, you allow them to feel that their views are understood, even if not agreed with, making it more likely that they will listen to you in the same way when it is your turn to speak.

- Using neutral language, maintaining a calm affect, and refraining from blaming statements allows others to hear and understand your views and concerns. Employing "emotional intelligence" is key to keeping this process constructive.

- Sharing all information and being very clear in defining the meaning of words helps to maximize mutual understanding and build trust.

- Get others to behave in the same constructive ways by reacting positively when they do and mildly negatively when they don't.

- The more you understand one another's views, the more likely you are to find mutually satisfying solutions.

Skill Building Activities

For Everyone	For Managers & Leaders
Assess your own Emotional Intelligence by taking one of the many surveys on this topic and asking for feedback from others who know you well:	Model the behaviors associated with Emotional Intelligence and active listening.
• How well do I seem to know myself and know what I'm feeling at any given time?	Convey expectations that everyone is to learn and master these behaviors.
• To what extent do I make good choices about how I do or don't express my feelings?	Make surfacing differences and employing constructive approaches to resolution a part of everyone's performance standard.
• How good am I at understanding other peoples' feelings?	
Expand your vocabulary of words that describe emotions.	
Increase your mindfulness by doing mini meditations and paying attention to your breathing.	
Practice active listening by:	
• Paraphrasing others' statements	
• Remaining open and neutral even if you disagree	
Identify a situation in which you can practice "diverge" in which the stakes are not too high.	
Ask someone to observe you and give you feedback.	

Chapter 10

Step 4: Co-Create

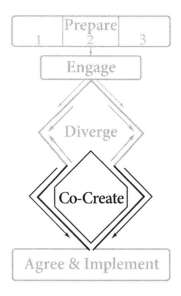

It is most effective at this point to be thinking of all of the parties as partners in the search for the best solution. With a commonly shared reframed statement of the issue to be resolved and the same understanding of all relevant information, including all parties' interests, everyone is able to view the problem "from above the cornfield" instead of through the narrow lens of self-interest. With that perspective, you are ready to work together in search of the best possible solutions to the problem.

There are three distinct parts of Co-Create:

- Establishing criteria for how you will ultimately evaluate possible solutions

- Generating all possible solutions

- Applying criteria to narrow the options, allowing for best solutions to become apparent

Establish Criteria

Though criteria will not be applied to eliminate options at this time, criteria in the form of "musts" and "wants" will be helpful in generating solutions that can be considered later. "Musts" are those things that the solution must do; that is to say, any solution that does not produce this outcome will not even be considered. "Wants" are those things that are desirable outcomes but are not deal-breakers; that is, some solutions may still be considered even though they do not achieve these desirable outcomes. Musts and wants really represent what is valued most. It is likely that many of these criteria have already been surfaced, though less explicitly, during the "Diverge" discussion as they reflect and are consistent with what have been identified as interests.

It is important for each person, or group of people representing a particular interest, to give some thought to how they want to articulate their musts and wants. There may be a temptation by some to overstate the musts by including items that are negotiable to some degree. Others may balk at the idea of being transparent about their criteria. This is a good time to reinforce the value and benefit of finding a solution that will serve everyone's interests as well as serving the organization. It is also helpful to introduce the idea of BATNA (best alternative to a negotiated agreement) and WATNA (worst alternative to a negotiated agreement.) These concepts, borrowed from the field of ADR (alternative dispute resolution), can help people rely more on their rational thinking than on their emotionally driven reasoning. As implied, it asks them to think about the most likely consequences of not reaching an agreement, both the best and the worst, for themselves and for the organization. Most often, there is a negative cost for everyone to not reaching a solution that is acceptable to all, as in the following example:

After the merger of three telecom companies, there was great disagreement about what management information system to use, with each company wanting to retain its own. The newly consolidated management team felt it was important for all of the IT directors to agree on one system rather than them having one imposed on them. After nearly a year they were still at an impasse, with the directors' inclination to protect their own team's interests as a major obstacle. As a result, other parts of the merger implementation could not go forward, work was delayed, costs were up due to duplications, customers were irritated, and staff morale was at an all time low. It was becoming clear to everyone that the ultimate consequence of not reaching an agreement would be a loss of customers and potentially the failure of the business. This realization led to the suggestion that the group work together to develop a list of criteria for what the system must do, must not do, or what it would be desirable for it to do. They were able to generate a list including many concerns that had been raised endlessly in previous discussions without reaching agreement: degree of ability to customize; degree of transparency; system security standards; cost, time, and training needed to implement; etc.

"Buy-in of their employees" moved to the lists of wants rather than musts. By defining the specific parameters they were willing to live with, they were able to identify some middle ground on each, leading to a list of possible system configurations and vendors. They also identified some things they were willing to accept even though they were not entirely desirable, e.g. opposition from some of their employees to certain features of a particular system.

Once individual lists of musts and wants are created and recorded, a combined list can be generated, and overlap or similarity and differences noted. The list of musts will be much smaller than the wants list. All are then encouraged to consider whether the things on the must list are truly non-negotiable and what impact that is likely to have on the outcome. Discussion and questions of clarification ensure that everyone understands the meaning of all the items. The list that is agreed to becomes a set of criteria against which possible solutions can be measured.

Generate All Possible Solutions

The second goal of Co-Create is to generate as many potential solutions to the situation as possible, with special focus on those that solve the problem for the long term, don't cause new problems, and satisfy multiple interests. Problem solving is considered the most complex of all human functions, requiring more complex logic and higher cognitive processes than other activities. Many people find it somewhat uncomfortable to engage in such cognitively challenging processes, often resorting to short-cut thinking and latching onto the first solution that comes to mind. The likelihood that everyone wants to get their own way makes it a challenge to keep people focused on solution-finding.

Using structured problem-solving methods helps to stimulate the best thinking and keep everyone engaged. Quickly review all of the information gathered to ensure that it is complete and that everyone agrees on its validity. If there are important pieces missing or there is significant distrust in the validity, it may be worth deferring this step until more information can be gathered, validated, and agreed upon. It is also worth taking the time to restate all interests to make sure that they are accurately represented and well understood by everyone. This also helps everyone stay focused on the big picture and rational rather than emotional considerations.

Next, select a specific process for generating solutions. The objective is to generate as many possibilities as can be conjured up by creative minds, resisting the temptation to jump directly to solutions that seem obvious to one individual. There is benefit in this because the best solutions most often appear when many different ideas are considered and combined or played off of one another in creative ways. Structured methods are employed to ensure that creativity is not discouraged or stifled as a result of subtle (or not so subtle) judgment and criticism, or as a result of the most vocal or assertive group members pushing through their own ideas.

Whichever methods are used, the ideas generated should be captured and recorded in a way that everyone can see simultaneously. There are now a number of electronic tools that can do this; these are great when everyone has a computer in front of them or a software tool has been purchased that allows everyone to see what is happening on their own computer or on a screen. Old-fashioned low-tech flip charts and markers work just fine for small groups.

Examples of creative problem-solving strategies include:

- Brainstorming
- Brain-Writing
- Nominal Group Process
- Piggy-Backing
- Problem Mapping
- Force Field Analysis
- Divide and Conquer
- Metaphorical Thinking
- Seeing Through Others' Lenses

Brainstorming simply invites all to think creatively and expansively, ignoring all judgments and evaluations, to come up with as many ideas as possible. All ideas are captured, no matter how wild or impractical.

Brain-Writing is the same as brainstorming except that people are given time to think and write the ideas down before they are captured. The benefit is that no one hears anyone else's ideas before generating their own, so they are less likely to be influenced.

Nominal Group Process builds on brain-writing by asking people to rank order their ideas, best first, then going around to each person getting their best ideas one idea at a time. If the idea has already been expressed they share the next one on the list. Keep going around until everyone's list of ideas has been exhausted. Often, there is considerable overlap in ideas. When people see that, they may begin to believe that there is more common ground than they had thought, making them more optimistic about finding a solution.

Piggy-Backing invites people to build on one another's ideas by combining them in different ways or seeing what happens when they take someone else's idea and take it to the next step, e.g. "If we did this and then did this, what would happen?"

Problem Mapping or Root Cause Analysis involves people in considering all the factors that impact the problem, either by creating it in the first place or by keeping it from being resolved. Fishbone mapping is one variation of this. The problem statement is put on a line, then everyone is invited to call out causes, which are written on diagonal lines connecting to the problem. These can be added to by extending to causes of the causes, and so forth, to create a complete map of all the factors and how they interact to keep the problem unresolved. This map is then used to generate more possible solutions, focusing on those that will solve the problem without causing or increasing other problems.

Force Field Analysis is a specific kind of problem mapping and root cause analysis that identifies forces that are driving the problem toward a resolution (driving forces) and those pushing against or preventing resolution (restraining forces). Once these are listed, forces on either side that are most significant are identified. This leads to proposals for solutions. (See example in Chapter 5.)

Divide and Conquer is used for problems that are revealed to be complex and derived from many related but distinct parts. In these cases, the problem can be divided into its parts and tackled separately. Solutions are then combined and examined to make sure they are not working at cross purposes.

Metaphorical Thinking is a way to help people break out of their usual linear or non-creative way of thinking. Employ a metaphor as a stand-in for the problem to generate novel thoughts. The software engineers in Chapters 4 to 6 might have been asked to think about their problem of how best to coordinate tasks and share resources to meet deadlines as doctors and nurses in an operating room, or train cars needing to climb a mountain. After generating ideas, people are asked to think about what ideas or new insights they can apply to their own problem.

Seeing Through Others' Lenses Imagine you are another person viewing the situation. Consider others who are involved or impacted in another way than the people who are working to resolve the issue. Consider what factors would be important to them and what would work for them.

Any of these can be used in part or in combinations. The choice depends on the complexity and type of issue to be resolved and the nature of the people participating. Choose the methods that you believe will generate the most creative thinking and useful solutions.

Once all ideas have been generated, everyone participates in narrowing the list by eliminating obvious duplications and combining ideas that are very similar or complementary. This is not the same as evaluating ideas. In fact, when everyone views all of the ideas, new, even more creative ideas can emerge.

Apply Criteria to Evaluate and Eliminate Solutions

Begin by reviewing the list of ideas to make sure all items are fully understood and clear to all, and that they are all distinct from one another. Number the items. Similarly, review the lists of musts and wants, making sure these are clear. More discussion may prompt some changes in the list of criteria.

Applying criteria can be done in several different ways, involving numerically weighted values for each criteria or something much more subjective like "voting" for preferred items. Either way, it must be transparent so that everyone trusts the process and observes how the results are reached. Whether numerically based or not, all methods involve a level of subjectivity combined with transparency.

Weighted Values involves assigning a numeric value for each criterion. Some common sense rules are applied to make it even-handed, e.g. each parties' "musts" should add up to the same number. Everyone must agree on the values assigned to each criterion. Each person or group applies the weighted values to each idea.

Subjective methods involve each group or person selecting the ideas they favor most, indicating their choices from most favored to least.

The following story exemplifies this methodology:

A restaurant and catering company had recently hired a new executive chef (Tom). Until hiring him, one of the owners (Irene) had performed all of the executive chef duties: preparing menus, generating shopping lists, managing inventory, overseeing all food preparation, managing and scheduling all kitchen staff, meeting with some high profile catering clients and talking with restaurant customers when time allowed. After just three months on the job, the tension between the new chef and the ex-chef/owner was palpable. Staff in the kitchen, the front of the house, and the sales team sensed that all was not well, partly because they were getting conflicting direction from Tom and Irene. The time taken up talking, speculating, and complaining about this was significant enough to impact performance.

At the prompting of the other owner and key employees, Tom and Irene agreed to meet to try to work things out. They agreed on a reframed problem: "How can we resolve our differences about menus and staffing so that Tom and Irene, and the kitchen staff can all perform their jobs successfully and the restaurant and catering businesses can succeed?"

After much sharing of information and discussion of each of their interests, they learned about one another's concerns:

Executive Chef Tom

- *Feels he has not been allowed the autonomy to create menus and new recipes as he was promised because Irene continues to be too involved*

- *Pressure to keep food costs down and use only certain vendors has interfered with his goal of building menus around seasonally available produce, which was one of the things they had all agreed on when he was hired*

- *"No overtime" policy for kitchen staff is leading to inadequate coverage at busiest times*

- *Servers are not knowledgeable enough to answer diners' questions about ingredients and preparation of menu items*

- *Catering customers are not being offered new menu items*

Ex-Chef/Owner Irene

- *Concerned that menus have not been getting done in time for the orders to get to produce, meat, and seafood suppliers by Monday afternoon as has always been the practice; feels this has caused some chaos and last minute changes*

- *Worried that some regular customers will not like the changes Tom is making to menus, especially elimination of some old favorites*

- *Believes certain employees drag their heels so that they will need overtime to complete their jobs; the "no overtime" policy was created to eliminate this and she does not want to change it; believes they should be pushed harder to get their work done in regular hours*

- *Feels executive chef should not be involved in catering meetings as sales team doesn't like it*

Tom's Musts & Wants

Musts

- *Able to use new recipes*

- *Able to use seasonal produce*

- *Adequate kitchen staff Thursday–Saturday prime prep time*

- *Kitchen staff understand they report to Tom, not Irene*

Wants

- *Time with servers to educate about new menu*

- *Be involved in catering sales meetings*

Irene's Musts & Wants

Musts

- *Food orders placed on time to avoid last minute disasters*

- *Kitchen staff able to get regular work done without needing overtime; labor costs contained*

- *Irene has final approval of menus*

Wants

- *Sales team runs catering sales meetings*

- *Be involved in menu planning*

During "Diverge," Irene had spoken about how the business had been based for many years on her own vision of the dining experience and how much she had enjoyed bringing that vision to life and creating a successful business. She had also enjoyed her mentoring relationship with kitchen staff, some of whom had moved on to become chefs at other establishments. Both Tom and she knew that the old vision had to be updated if the restaurant was to succeed, but it became more apparent that it was still difficult for Irene to let go of the old ways of doing things and her role in it. It also became more clear to Irene that Tom was truly passionate about his belief in the new approach to food based on seasonal ingredients and that he probably wouldn't stay anywhere that would not allow him to apply the philosophy.

When Tom and Irene stepped back to assess the situation based on what they had just learned, they came to the following conclusions:

- *There are plenty of positive "driving" forces in the situation: Both want restaurant to succeed; both agree that Tom has the skills to run the kitchen; new younger people moving into neighborhood like the idea of food prepared with fresh products; some staff are interested in learning new cooking methods from Tom; both agree that a more engaged staff is likely to be a more efficient staff.*

- *There are also some negative "restraining" forces: Some regular customers may not like menu changes; the restaurant's financial picture is precarious; the sales team, which works on commission, is adamant about Tom not being too closely involved in catering sales.*

There are several levels of the conflict:

- Facts/Information: Some information is missing, like the impact of working with new vendors on cost and other variables; customer preferences cannot be known without trying out new things; Tom may not know all of the details of the financials.

- Processes & Practices: This is the heart of the conflict, e.g. how decisions will be made with regard to kitchen staffing and menu changes.

- Goals, Objectives, Priorities: Both have the overarching goal of wanting the restaurant to succeed in terms of customer satisfaction and financial viability; they differ on priority relative to menu items.

- Behavior, History, Feelings: Irene's feelings of becoming obsolete and having less position power in her own restaurant are elements that probably had not been expressed or acknowledged; Tom may be feeling a little betrayed.

- Values, Beliefs: They share many of these but Tom's strong value on cooking with fresh ingredients is not as strongly held by Irene; both probably understand that if the restaurant cannot succeed by following his philosophy he will eventually leave.

- Organizational Culture: The restaurant's traditional top-down hierarchy will probably change under Tom's management, as he wants to build his staff's engagement and motivation by allowing them to learn and be more involved in the work of the kitchen.

The potential for an integrative "win-win" solution seems high.

- *They agreed to brainstorm ideas and they also agreed that it might be useful to think about the situation through the lens of the kitchen staff, the sales staff, and the dining customers. Ultimately, they came up with a list of ideas, including:*

- *Weekly tastings to learn about new menu items and about cooking with seasonal ingredients for staff created and managed by Tom: mandatory for servers, all else welcome to attend. Irene will attend whenever possible.*

- *The menu is a jointly developed blend of old items known to be customer favorites and newer innovative dishes, to be agreed upon seasonally for regular menu and weekly for specials with Irene having final approval.*

- *Tom explores new vendors/suppliers with more flexible delivery schedules who can provide fresh produce and seafood at competitive costs. They will work together on pricing new items.*

- *Tom and Irene work together to review current kitchen staffing, and also work together on new scheduling plans and policies for kitchen staff.*

- *They institute performance management systems for kitchen staff emphasizing the need to get work done in timely way.*

- *Kitchen staff will be offered opportunities to come up with their own ideas for new dishes and to oversee prep if interested.*

- *The sales team will be consulted on how they could involve Tom in catering menus.*

Tom and Irene assessed the ideas based on their earlier list of criteria. They agreed to implement some of the ideas right away, some at a later date as time allowed, and some provisionally to see how they worked and be willing to re-assess and adjust.

Key Learning Points

- Jointly establishing criteria for evaluating possible solutions ensures that all interests will be considered in arriving at the ultimate resolution. This important step both continues to build trust and provides a helpful tool for narrowing choices.

- Resolution-seeking is essentially a creative activity that requires structured methods to allow people to break through their tendencies to be evaluative and to jump too quickly to easy answers.

- Applying criteria only after many possible solutions have been generated ensures that the solutions are both high quality (i.e. they solve the problem in a lasting way without creating new issues and are good for the organization) and acceptable to all.

Skill Building Activities

For Everyone	For Managers & Leaders
Thinking of a real situation in which there are differences, check in with yourself about what a truly good solution would have to include. Make a list, then go back and separate the list into "musts" and "wants."	Create opportunities for groups and teams to work together to solve problems creatively and collaboratively.
Work on building creativity by using some of the tools mentioned in this chapter.	Create cross-functional task groups to address particularly complex problems. Provide the resources they need, including time and space.
Spend time building creativity through other creative endeavors like puzzles that force you to think broadly and outside the usual.	Encourage others to think outside the box; stay open and be willing to change an approach when it is warranted.

Chapter 11

Step 5: Agree and Implement

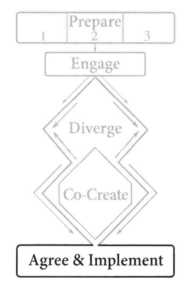

Reaching Agreements

In many of the situations we have encountered, by the time participants have worked through the first four steps, it has become obvious to all that several potential solutions satisfy most, if not all, of the criteria. Even though the "Co-Create" step does not specifically include reaching agreement on solutions, it is often the case that there is tacit agreement about what things are going to happen, as we just saw in the case of Tom and Irene. This doesn't necessarily mean all will be smooth sailing.

While agreement is, of course, the ultimate goal, it is also important to ensure that what is being agreed to is actually implementable and will solve the problem in an enduring way. It is possible for people to over-promise in the moment or to not consider all of the ramifications of what they have agreed to. Further exploration is called for.

Review and Apply Criteria to Proposed Solutions

Even though there may be some solutions that have become obvious and acceptable to all, it is a good idea to review the criteria that were developed during Co-Create and consider the proposed solutions against them. Doing this will help to ensure that everyone is applying rational, logical thinking to the decision-making process and not being influenced by other factors. From time to time, we have seen individuals get carried along by the emotions that can be generated by feelings of relief or gratitude that the problem is actually going to be solved. In these instances, people can unintentionally agree to something that, upon later reflection, they regret.

Reviewing the criteria together, then considering all of the possible solutions that have been generated allows everyone to see how far they have come. As they discuss and consider each possible solution and evaluate how well it meets the criteria, they can decide which are in the best interest of the organization and for themselves, in the long run as well as near term. This discussion allows everyone to make informed and rational decisions about where it makes sense to compromise, where there are possibilities for complementary options, and where there are truly collaborative solutions that serve all interests.

Defining Agreement

What does it mean to agree? Agreement doesn't necessarily call for everyone to unequivocally or even enthusiastically endorse a solution or believe that it is the best one. Agreement can be thought of as lying on a continuum that ranges from enthusiastic support to some degree of disagreement with a willingness to support. Anything less than the latter is not acceptable.

For most situations, having most people be somewhere in the middle is enough.

Degree of agreement needed to make a solution work will vary, situation to situation. For example, in instances for which many people will need to be actively involved in implementing a solution, it is more important to have greater levels of agreement. For others, where support can be passive, lower levels of agreement may not affect the outcome.

The "Eighty—Twenty Rule"

It is not unusual for some issues to not have obvious solutions and to remain unresolved. Typically, about one-fifth, or twenty percent, of the concerns fall into this category. A choice can be made to address these more challenging issues now in a more traditional negotiation, continue to try to find mutually satisfying solutions, or table them until some of the agreements can be implemented. In some situations, successfully implementing the actions that are agreed to first generates enough optimism and good will that agreement on the more challenging concerns can be reached later on.

Expanding Options by Broadening the Problem Frame and Deepening Understanding of Interests

Addressing parts of the problem that appear irresolvable calls for some extra effort. Is a compromise called for? Should one person just give in? Or is it possible to arrive at a truly good solution for everyone by re-examining some earlier understandings?

For Tom and Irene, the issue of whether overtime for kitchen staff could be scheduled and paid at a higher hourly rate remained unresolved. A decision had to be made for the short term, even if it was only temporary. They could choose to look for an expedient compromise, settling on some number of hours of overtime for some employees at a certain rate of pay that was in between both of their real wants. This would solve the problem for the short term, but would probably not solve the underlying problem that each of them cared most about, i.e. Tom needing more help during the busiest prep times and Irene's concerns about overall costs. It could also cause confusion for the staff.

Another choice would be for one party to simply give in for the sake of the relationship. Though also expedient, they felt that either way—no overtime allowed or all the overtime Tom thought was needed—would not provide the best solution for the restaurant and might undermine their tentative, newly improved working relationship. Instead, they decided to try to build on their improved understanding of the entire situation and of one another's interests and motivations to arrive at a solution that would be good for all. They started to talk again about the way they had framed the problem and wondered if it could now be made broader and more inclusive of all of their interests.

This can be an effective strategy in moving even the most intractable differences toward resolution. By enlarging or shifting the boundaries of the problem being addressed to include more perspectives, more interests and considerations can be brought into the solution-seeking process and, ultimately, more solutions can be found that are acceptable to all.

For Tom and Irene, this may mean adding the elements of updating the menu to attract new clientele and the need to sustain a certain level of profitability while the transition is occurring. In place of the initial reframed statement "How can we resolve our differences about menus and staffing so that Tom and Irene, and the kitchen staff, can all perform their jobs successfully, and the restaurant and catering businesses can succeed?" they might now ask "How can we transition the menu to attract new clientele while ensuring consistent quality for our customers (old and new) and sustained profitability?" With this new question, they will need to look more closely at the impact of any paid overtime on profitability. By agreeing on some assumptions about Tom's ability to bring in new business quickly based on promoting the new menu, they may be able to agree to do a trial run of allowing overtime for a few key employees who will come in to learn the new menu items and food preparation techniques.

A Deeper Understanding of Interests

Another way to generate more and better possible solutions is to exchange more information about interests—what is really important to each person and why. This can lead to the discovery of things that one person can do to help the other satisfy interests without giving up anything themselves.

> As Irene learned more about the reasons behind Tom's wanting to cook with seasonal foods and the experience he brought, she became more comfortable with the idea of giving him more opportunities to shape the menu and source the food. Still wary of raising costs, Irene agreed to a plan for Tom to take control of a limited number of menu items while closely tracking and documenting costs. As Tom understood more about Irene's sense of loss in having a less central role in the restaurant, they came up with the idea that she should hostess on some of the nights that her oldest customers tended to come in.

There may still be some concerns that are not so easily resolved and must be negotiated the old-fashioned way—horse-trading: "I'll do 'x' if you do 'y'" or "I'll take half and you take half." These solutions are not ideal because no one is really getting all they want and they may not be the best possible solutions for the organization, but they may be the best that can be agreed to at this time. Ultimately, when other solutions are implemented successfully, these can be revisited.

Addressing the Underlying Issues

The problem has been addressed at the level that is, most practically speaking, the easiest to resolve. This means that there may well be other, deeper issues, involving values or emotions, that have not been addressed. Has the relationship improved enough through the process that these other kinds of issues can now be addressed or, alternatively, be put aside for the long run in order to make the agreements work?

In the case of Tom and Irene, their discussions led them to much greater understanding of one another's interests, needs, wants, and motivations. As a result, they also have developed greater trust in and for one another. It may now be possible for Irene to share more about the emotions she feels about her role and history with the restaurant and how difficult it is to let go. Tom may be willing to share more about his own history and his aspirations. The more this level of understanding can be reached, the more likely the agreements will be implemented successfully and future issues will be dealt with constructively.

Putting Aside Emotions

Many emotions may still remain for both Tom and Irene, including fear, sadness, frustration, bitterness and more. At the beginning of their relationship, before their discussions had helped them build trust for one another and even (perhaps) respect, these emotions were much harder for them to put aside. Acting on the basis of these alone did not lead to constructive discussion. Though still difficult, each now has the capacity for an internal dialogue:

> *Irene: I have been so afraid to let go of control of the restaurant, partly because I'm afraid of what will happen to me if it isn't financially successful. But I'm realizing too that it's just as much because I'm going to lose a part of myself, a part that helped me feel good about myself and define who I am. That part is making me really sad.*

I know now that I have to let Tom have more of what he needs to stay and make it work, but it's still going to be hard. I hope he understands that.

Tom: I've been pushing hard to have the autonomy I need to show my talent here and prove that I can make it work. I've felt angry and frustrated and a little insulted that Irene wouldn't just let me run with it, but if I'm really honest, I know that it's a risk. I may have been a bit too demanding and expected too much too soon. I have great ideas and strong skills but there's plenty I don't know. Irene has been doing this a long time and even though some of her ideas are outdated, she knows a lot about the restaurant business. I hope we can find a way to work together.

And this can lead to an external dialogue:

Tom: "I'm really hopeful that we're going to be able to work together now. As long as we can keep talking through our different views and respecting each others' experience and expertise, we can do it. I want you to know that I do respect you and what you've created here, and that I still have things to learn from you. I know now that you understand how much I want the restaurant to succeed and that I really do have something of value to bring to it."

Irene: "It really makes me feel good to hear you say that you might still have some things to learn from me. This has been my life's work, so I sure hope I've learned a few things! And of course, I wouldn't have hired you in the first place (and put up with some of your arrogance!) if I hadn't known how talented you are. I think we're going to be ok!"

Several important things have happened here. First, both Tom and Irene have allowed themselves to acknowledge and accept their own emotions, even a few that were a little difficult to embrace. They've named those emotions and been able to put them aside for the sake of the business and the relationship between them that is crucial to its success. Finally, they've each worked to understand the other's perspective and have validated the other's worth. As a result, they've created a shared optimism that will carry them forward.

There will be more challenging issues they must address, but they have a much greater chance now to resolve them constructively. This new level of collaboration will be felt by everyone, including staff and customers. All of this would most likely not have happened had they not addressed the substantive issues first.

Implementing Agreements

With the hard work of reaching agreements done for now, there is a last step to ensure that actions will be taken, practices, process and behaviors changed, and problems solved.

The Devil is in the Details: Clarify, Define, Assign

Agreements are frequently stated in broad terms and in language that everyone assumes is understood in the same way by all. Without clarifying meanings and ensuring similar understandings, agreements can unravel quickly. Take the time to review each item that has been agreed to and define precisely what it means in terms of actions and how it is to be carried out: what is to be done, by whom, and by when.

> *Tom and Irene agreed that new policies would be put in place for kitchen staff, including scheduling, overtime, performance management, and growth opportunities. In order to implement this agreement, they agreed on the following:*
>
> *• Tom would draw up a proposed set of policies that he believed would be effective in motivating kitchen staff and would share it with Irene in two weeks (specific date and time), including an overall management philosophy and cost/benefit assessment;*

- *Tom would outline the program he wanted to put in place to offer kitchen staff opportunities for growth and development;*

- *There would be no mention of any of this to kitchen staff until Tom and Irene had both agreed and signed off on it;*

- *Once the new policies and programs were in place, Tom would be in charge of managing it and the staff.*

Monitor and Correct

With any new initiative, there is a potential for imperfection, if not outright failure. How will you know if things are going as planned, if outcomes are as anticipated, or if there are un- intended consequences? New programs and processes must be monitored and outcomes documented to keep track of their impact, positive and negative. It is best to be clear about how this monitoring will be done, who will do it, and who else needs to know the results. There should also be understanding of what will happen if something needs to be changed or reconsidered.

> *Upon instituting the new management policies, Tom and Irene agreed that they would meet with the bookkeep- er/accountant to come up with a way to monitor labor costs month-to-month. They also agreed to work toward creating a new benchmark for receipts vs. food + labor that would enable them to make better decisions about menus and staffing in the future.*

Key Learning Points

- Typically, 80% of the issues are very close to being resolved by the time this step is reached; apply criteria to ensure that the solutions that appear to be most agreeable truly meet them.

- Doing a deep and thorough review of the situation, the problem frame, and all of the interests can lead to a new level of understanding and an opportunity to expand the options.

- Some of the remaining issues can be tabled for later until agreements are implemented, often leading to greater belief in the process and trust in one another.

- Define agreements, clarify terms and identify specific actions and responsibilities in order to successfully implement them; monitor results and plan for corrections.

Skill Building Activities

For Everyone	For Managers & Leaders
Think back to situations in which you have agreed to a solution to a problem. Reflect on: • Have you ever agreed to something that you regretted or couldn't live up to? • Have you ever had someone else renege on an agreement? • If either of these has happened, what could you have done differently to produce a better outcome? • Was the agreement clear enough that everyone knew exactly what they were promising to do? How could it have been made clearer?	Celebrate successes in problem solving and conflict resolution, especially those in which people worked collaboratively and creatively. Publicize and communicate these widely. Don't allow collaborative problem solving to be an excuse to avoid making hard decisions. Sometimes it really is up to a leader to lead the way.

Chapter 12

Yes, But…

As you've read these pages and thought about applying the concepts to your own challenging situations, you have probably had some "yes, but…" moments. In this conclusion, we'll try to read your minds and give you some responses and suggestions.

Yes, But… I'm Not Sure That What is in the Organization's Interest is Truly in my Interest

This may, in some situations, be the case. At some point, or even at many points along the way, you should be asking yourself whether this is where you want to be for the long haul. This personal quest is yours to grapple with.

> Tom, the executive chef, knew that the job at Irene's restaurant was a stepping stone to larger things. He saw this as an opportunity to develop his skills, both as chef and manager, and to build his resume. Even though it would not be his home forever, it was in his best long-term interests to help Irene make the restaurant a success.

It is in your interest for the organization to be successful and for you to be successful in it. There is a larger question worth pondering, though: How does anyone decide where, among all of the groups and associations to which we belong, our best interests lie? For other animals, biology wins out and the choice always has to do with survival of self and offspring. Human animals seem to make things more complicated.

Family of origin, nuclear family, extended family, race, ethnicity, community, city, state, nation, religion; all are part of our identity. And we haven't even begun to consider occupation-related groups; professional and trade associations, unions, or other organizations. When framing interests, some of these may well be incompatible.

This is a matter of personal conscience to be considered in the context of whatever situation you are addressing. Perhaps most relevant here is the question of whether your efforts at constructive resolution building have a good chance of being rewarded by the organization. It will be up to you to position yourself and your good work as a collaborator in such a way that it brings you positive recognition. Better still, you will be helping to move the organization toward a culture of collaboration.

Yes, But... the People I'm Dealing With are Impossible

Or self-righteous, or malicious, or obnoxious... fill in the word. Yes, our worlds are filled with all kinds of people whom we feel are difficult or just different. Some people are filled with an intense need to be "right;" others are narrow in their way of thinking and, yes, there probably are some who really do want to do harm.

> One of the software engineers responsible for delivering updates was particularly resistant to modifying his behavior in any way to accommodate the needs of others or even to really listen to what others had to say. As the other engineers responsible for delivering finished software to production began to work together more effectively, this one person became an obstacle to improvement. The others, some of whom were his friends, tried to give him feedback and help him see that his cooperation was needed and that, ultimately, his job might be in jeopardy if he could not work more collaboratively. Eventually, this man confided with another about problems he was having in his personal life. He was advised to get help. Though his level of cooperation did not change immediately, he became less negative and less of an obstacle.

We've tried to equip you with some tools that will help you get a good outcome without allowing yourself to be taken advantage of or giving in to solutions that do not serve the greater good. Apply tit-for-tat thinking, allow others to have their views heard and acknowledged, express your own views respectfully, and stay open and creative. These approaches and behaviors will be contagious.

If at any point you feel you are about to lose control of the process or are in danger of agreeing to things that are not in the organization's best interests, or in yours, call a time out. Seek out a wise confidant who can help you figure out how to get it back on track.

Yes, But… the Emotions Can Override All the Rest

It's hard! But it is possible to train yourself to manage your emotions so that they do not get the best of you. And when you model calm and collected, others are impacted in a good way.

> *The magazine editor who had tried for months to gain permission to increase headcount in her organization was about ready to boil over with frustration. By nature an emotionally demonstrative person, she realized, with coaching, that her expressive behavior was getting in the way of having people hear her words and take her seriously. When she had the opportunity to make her argument directly to the CEO, she worked very hard to present the facts calmly, slowing down her speech and listening to others without interrupting and without accusations. The results were so positive she could barely believe what happened and—as important—she felt heard for the first time.*

Emotional intelligence and mindfulness—the ability to be in the present and observe your own thoughts and feelings and those of others without making judgments about them—take practice and discipline. If they don't come naturally to you, learn more about how to develop them, first by reading and/or taking a class, then by practicing.

Demonstrating your humanity by visibly struggling with your emotions is not a bad thing, as long as you are able to express yourself non-emotionally. Naming what you are feeling and verbalizing it is the best way to defuse it and to model for others that feelings are ok, but acting them out is not.

Yes, But… It Doesn't Really Work Like That in Real Life

You're right! Nothing is ever going to happen in the orderly way we might seem to be suggesting. Facts don't line up; people don't show up or someone unexpected does; not everyone in the room wants to do it your way, or some other completely unanticipated event occurs.

> *Don, the head of sales, was able to get his colleague to hear and acknowledge the validity of his approach to partnering with vendors who would be with them for the long haul. Shortly after their initial agreement and before they were able to put the changed criteria in place, the colleague left the company. His replacement was someone Don knew as hard-headed and less inclined to compromise with others. Don knew it would take time to build a relationship and try again to get agreement on the program he believed would be best for the company. He was frustrated, but not about to give up.*

It is only possible to follow the steps as best you can and to work with the situation as it occurs. We don't promise perfect outcomes. We do promise that if you adhere to the principles, practice the skills, and model the behaviors, the outcome will be substantially better than if your didn't do these things.

Summary Table: Five Steps For Resolving Differences Constructively

STEP	PURPOSE	OBJECTIVES	ESSENTIAL APPROACHES AND SKILLS
PREPARE—PART 1: UNDERSTAND THE SITUATION	Gather as much information as possible about the entire situation, without evaluating or making judgments	Practice taking the "view from the balcony"; being an objective observer seeing the whole big picture	Curiosity
			Objectivity; Ability to remain unbiased
		Gather facts, distinguishing fact from opinion	Observation skills
		Learn about others' views and perspectives, and the way they think about the situation	Forming open-ended questions
			Information gathering
		Discover and understand multiple viewpoints	Knowledge of the organization

Summary Table: Five Steps For Resolving Differences Constructively

STEP	PURPOSE	OBJECTIVES	ESSENTIAL APPROACHES AND SKILLS
PREPARE—PART 2: ANALYZE THE INFORMATION FOR CLUES	View the information all together to look for patterns and connections, and generate insights Frame the situation as an interconnected system	Apply analytic tools to more precisely understand the situation Generate a preliminary strategy and approach to resolving the issues	Knowledge of analytic tools, including: Force Field Analysis Integrative Assessment Level Analysis Ability to see patterns, analyze information Objectivity Neutrality Strategic Thinking Optimism—Ability to focus on positive outcomes

Summary Table: Five Steps For Resolving Differences Constructively

STEP	PURPOSE	OBJECTIVES	ESSENTIAL APPROACHES AND SKILLS
PREPARE—PART 3: KNOW YOURSELF, KNOW OTHERS	Apply the principles of human behavior when dealing with differences to become more aware of your own and others' predispositions and motivations	Become aware of your own default style of behavior when dealing with a difference	Knowledge of theories of human behavior related to needs, motivation, and conflict
		Increase awareness of what is at stake for you in the situation	Thomas Kilmann Conflict Mode
			Myers Briggs Type Indicator
		Identify your real interests— what is most important to you in the situation	Sources of Identity
			Motivation
			Self-awareness
		Use your knowledge and awareness to determine the most likely predispositions, motivations, and interests of others involved	Reflection
			Objectivity
			Neutrality
			Skills of observation
			Empathy—being able to see another's point of view

Summary Table: Five Steps For Resolving Differences Constructively

STEP	PURPOSE	OBJECTIVES	ESSENTIAL APPROACHES AND SKILLS
DIVERGE	Identify and acknowledge all views, interests, concerns, and feelings of everyone involved	Make it possible for everyone to understand the interests, views, experiences, and perspectives of all involved Communicate your own interests, views, and concerns Allow everyone to feel that their views and experiences have been heard and understood Allow everyone to have all of the same information about the situation, including facts and opinions Encourage constructive and collaborative behavior by modeling and reinforcement	Interpersonal communication skills Active listening Speaking with neutral language Speaking to be understood rather than convince Suspending judgment "Bracketing"—ability to hold multiple and opposing views simultaneously Managing emotions Ability to remain open, delay closure Empathy Patience

Summary Table: Five Steps For Resolving Differences Constructively

STEP	PURPOSE	OBJECTIVES	ESSENTIAL APPROACHES AND SKILLS
CO-CREATE	Working together and considering all the information, generate multiple possible solutions that can resolve the reframed issue and evaluate them relative to established criteria	Establish criteria for how possible solutions will be evaluated Generate as many possible solutions as you can Apply criteria to narrow the options	Inventiveness, creativity Tolerance for uncertainty Big-picture, long-term thinking Problem solving methods Active listening Suspending judgment Bracketing Facilitation Collaboration Engagement Patience

Summary Table: Five Steps For Resolving Differences Constructively

STEP	PURPOSE	OBJECTIVES	ESSENTIAL APPROACHES AND SKILLS
AGREE AND IMPLEMENT	Select and agree on those solutions that best meet the criteria, solve the problems and that can be agreed upon	Review and re-establish agreed-upon criteria If necessary, work to deepen understanding of all interests in order to broaden the problem frame Arrive at some level of agreement on at least eighty percent of the issues Agree on an approach and time frame for addressing remaining issues	Collaboration Empathy Active listening Intense focus and commitment to the process Facilitation Optimism about the outcome Decision making Consensus building Letting go

Acknowledgments

It would impossible to recall and name all of the individuals, institutions, and organizations that have shaped these ideas and my thinking about how to help people resolve organizational differences. I will try to name a few and thank them here, knowing that it will just scratch the surface.

Dr Max Goodson, a professor in the Educational Policy Department at the University of Wisconsin, where I was working on my doctorate, was the first to expose me to the theory of 'Differentiation and Re-Integration'. Not only was he an early teacher, but he allowed me to work on his consulting team with school systems as clients, bringing theory to action. He also insisted I attend NTL (National Training Laboratory, then an offshoot of NEA, now the NTL Institute for Applied Behavioral Science). Between Dr Goodson and NTL, I was hooked on helping organizations apply social and behavioral science.

Brief encounters with other early Organizational Development practitioners, including Ron Lippitt, Marv Weisbord, Dick Beckhard, and so many others taught me about organizations and instilled the belief that we have many tools to help them become more effective. Charlie and Edie Seashore and all at NTL, especially, kept me from feeling isolated in my practice. Later, working with Kathy Dannemiller was an experience full of tremendous learning about how large, disparate groups can learn to collaborate and build consensus.

Zena Zumeta provided my first instruction in mediation, which was invaluable, and broadened my thinking about all the tools and approaches that could be applied to working with organizations. The mediator community of which I became a part of in Maryland was a wonderful professional home-base for many years. It was a privilege to take part in the growth of Maryland Council of Dispute Resolution (MCDR) and see the flourishing of Maryland Mediation and Conflict Resolution Office (MACRO) under the leadership of Rachel Wohl.

Joining forces with my partner, John Shorb, who brought with him years of learning about how effective organizations really work while a manager at Procter & Gamble, was probably the luckiest thing that ever happened to me. We continue to make a great team and learn from each other's approaches, points of view, and toolkits.

Our many clients, some of whom you've read about in the examples in the book (and who shall remain nameless here for the sake of confidentiality), helped me to learn what works and what doesn't. I thank them all and hope they benefited from our intervention.

A huge thank you to those who encouraged me to write this book, especially my colleague and friend, Dave Osborne, and those colleagues who took the time to read early versions of the manuscript and give me thoughtful feedback and comments: Louise Phipps-Senft and David Kiel.

And finally, my tireless editor, Shelagh Aitken, whose precise eye is spectacular and whose grasp of my sometimes muddled meanings has been invaluable. Likewise, illustrator Angela Dowd, who has had an uncanny way of reading my mind and depicting the concepts visually. Thank you both!

Thank you to everyone who has read the book and to all of you who will find a way to use some of the approaches in your lives and in your work!

References

Blake, R. R. and J. S. Mouton, *Solving Costly Organizational Conflicts*. San Francisco: Jossey-Bass, 1984.

Deutsch, M., *The Resolution of Conflict: Constructive and Destructive Processes*. New Haven: Yale University Press, 1973.

Dictionary of Conflict Resolution. Compiled and edited by D. Yarn. San Francisco: Jossey-Bass, 1999.

Fisher, R. and W. Ury, *Getting to Yes; Negotiating Without Giving In*. Penguin Books, 1983.

Goleman, Daniel, *Working with Emotional Intelligence*. Bantam Books, 1998.

Johnson, D. W. and R. Johnson, *Cooperation and Competition: Theory and Research*. Edina Minnesota Interaction, 1989.

Johnson, D. W. and R. Johnson, "The Value of Intellectual Opposition" in *The Handbook of Conflict Resolution, Theory and Practice*. Edited by M. Deutsch and P. Coleman. San Francisco: Jossey-Bass, 2000, pages 65–85.

Lewin, Kurt. *Field Theory in Social Science*. New York: Harper & Row, 1951. Reissued by University of Chicago Press, 1976.

Lewin, Kurt. *Resolving Social Conflicts*. New York: Harper & Row, 1948. Reissued by University of Chicago Press, 1976.

Maslow, Abraham. *Motivation and Personality, 2nd edition*, New York & London: Harper & Row, 1954.

Pruitt, D. G. and S. A. Lewis, "Development of Integrative Solutions in Bilateral Negotiation," *Journal of Personality and Social Psychology*, 1975, vol. 31, pp. 621–633.

Ridley, Matt. *The Origins of Virtue*, Viking, 1996.

Pruitt, D. G. and J. Z. Rubin, *Social Conflict: Escalation, Stalemate and Settlement*, New York: Random House, 1986.

Thomas, K. and R. Kilmann, *Thomas–Kilmann Conflict Mode Instrument*, Xicom, 1974.

Additional Recommended Reading

Block, Peter. *The Answer to How is Yes*, Berrett-Koehler Publishers, San Francisco, 2002.

Cornelius, Randolph R. *The Science of Emotion; Research and Tradition in the Psychology of Emotion*, Prentice-Hall, NJ, 1996.

Crosby, Robert. *Cultural Change in Organizations*, Robert P. Crosby, 2011.

DeBono, Edward. *Six Thinking Hats*, MICA Management Resources, 1985.

Havener, Cliff. *Meaning, The Secret of Being Alive*, Beaver Pond Press, Minnesota, 1999.

Jacobs, Robert W. *Real Time Strategic Change*, Berrett-Koehler, San Francisco, 1994.

Kline, Nancy. *More Time To Think; A Way of Being In The World*, Fisher King Publishing, Pool-in-Wharfedale, England, 2009.

Mayer, Bernard. *The Dynamics of Conflict Resolution*, Jossey-Bass, San Francisco, 2000.

Mindell, A. *Sitting In The Fire: Large Group Transformation Using Conflict and Diversity*, Lao Tse Press, Portland Oregon, 1995

Pink, Daniel H. *Drive, The Surprising Truth About What Motivates Us*, Riverhead Books, New York, 2009.

Schein, Edgar, *Organizational Culture and Leadership*, Jossey-Bass, San Francisco, 1985.

Stone, D., B. Patton, and S. Heen, *Difficult Conversations: How To Discuss What Matters Most*, Penguin Books, New York, 1999.

Watkins, J.M., and B. J. Mohr, *Appreciative Inquiry; Change at the Speed of Imagination*, Jossey-Bass/Pfeiffer, 2011.

Weisbord, Marvin R. *Productive Workplaces; Organizing and Managing for Dignity, Meaning, and Community*, Jossey-Bass, San Francisco, 1987.

Weisbord, Marvin R. *Discovering Common Ground*, Berrett-Koehler, San Francisco, 1992.

Ury, William. *Getting to Peace: Transforming Conflict at Home, at Work, and in the World*, Viking, 1999.

Made in the USA
Middletown, DE
03 January 2017